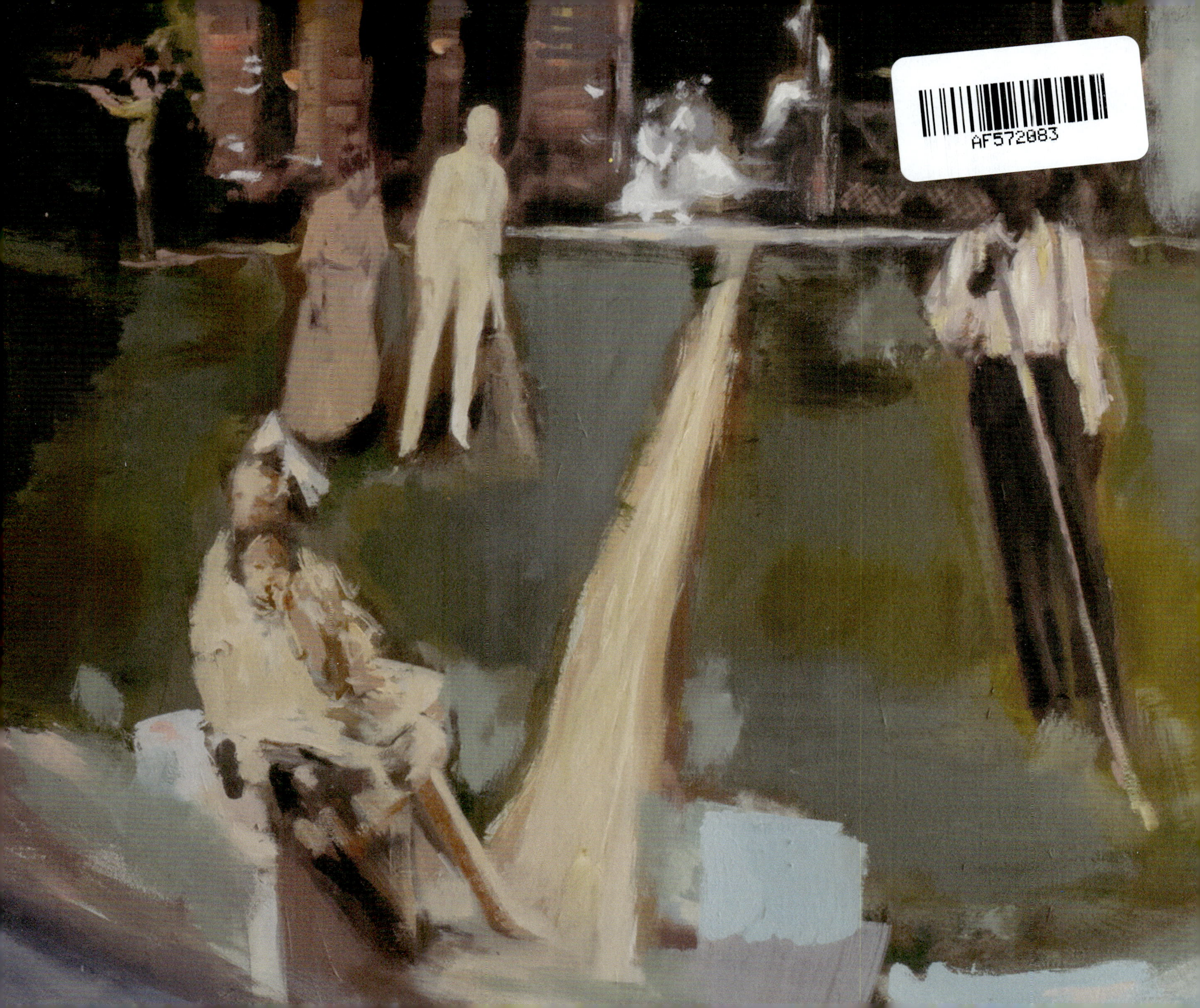

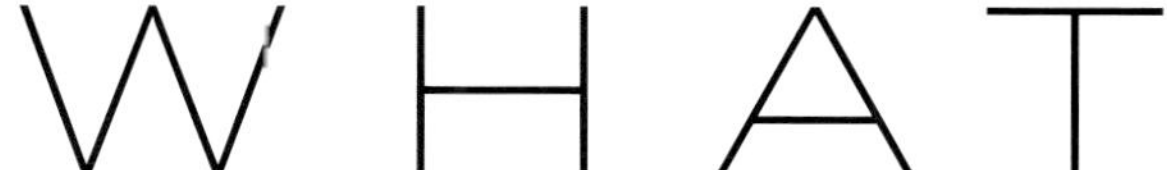

BECAME OF
DR. SMITH

NOAH SATERSTROM
MEGAN HINES, PHD

With contributions by
AMY FORBES, PHD, AND PATRICK HOPKINS, PHD
TIMOTHY HYMAN, RA
ANN PATCHETT

MISSISSIPPI MUSEUM OF ART
JACKSON

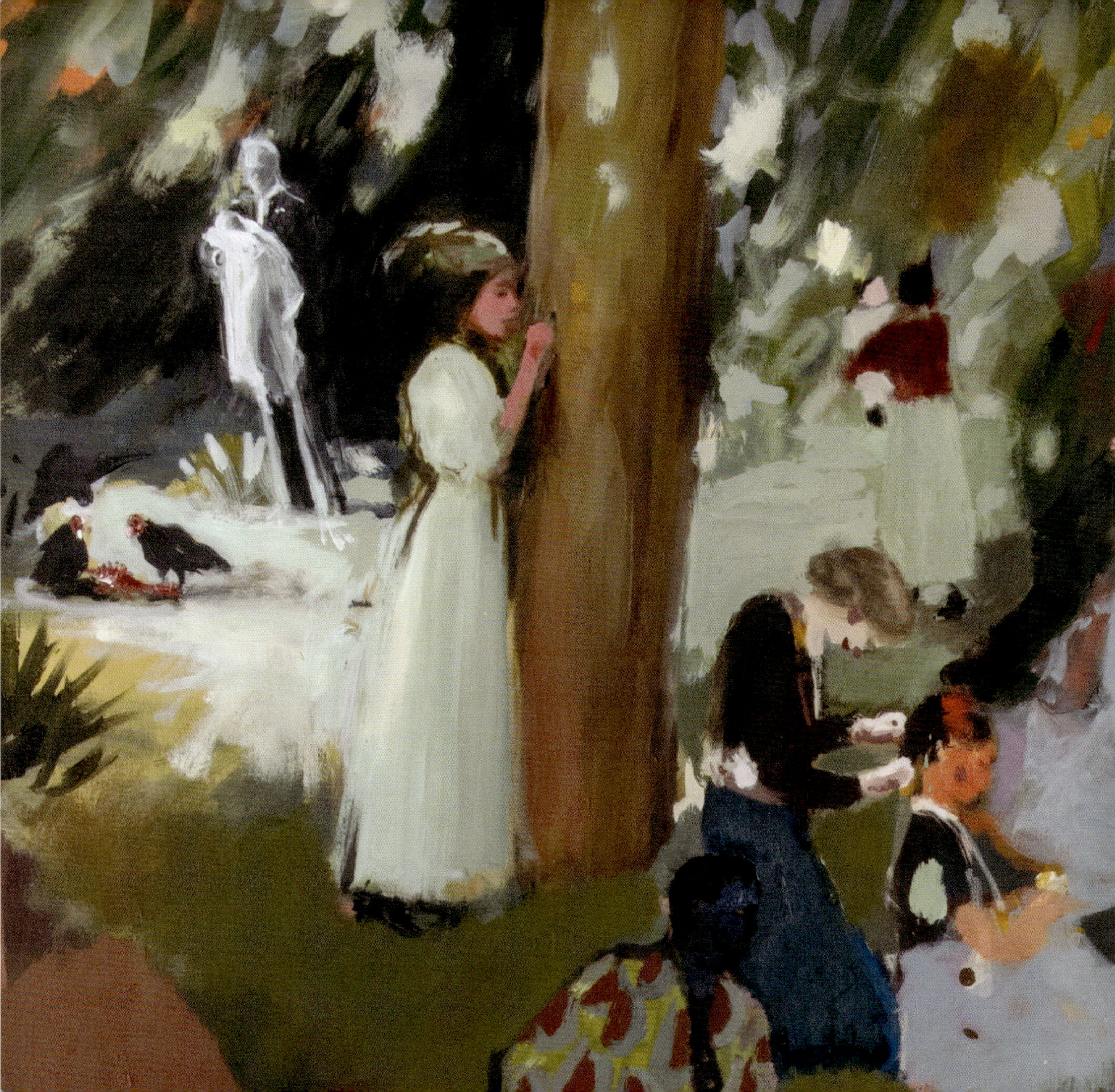

CONTENTS

FOREWORD

IN EARLY 2018, NOAH SATERSTROM SPOKE AT A MISSISSIPPI MUSEUM OF ART SYMPOSIUM when his painting *Road to Shubuta* (2016) was on display. I was struck by the artist's honest confrontation with his family's role in a history most Southerners suppress at best, or deny, at worst. It was almost as though Noah was daring the past to reveal itself so he could determine its place of residence inside him, so he could bully it out from within and shine the direct and often brutal gaze of the artist onto it.

After the symposium, he asked to meet with me, and I heard for the first time the story of Dr. Smith. Noah left my office, "accidentally" met Stephen Parks, the state librarian, and then met with my good friend Lida Gibson, who was working intently on the nascent Asylum Hill Project at the University of Mississippi Medical Center. From that point on, the past had nowhere to hide. It was no match for the strength and courage of Noah's character, and the loose threads of the story were no match for Noah's ability to weave a tapestry that would shame even Arachne.

I could tell from our initial conversation, before Noah learned much of what he now knows about his great-grandfather, that he would finish a monumental painting about this history, and that the Museum needed to show it. What I didn't know then was the force driving Noah—his insistence on reclaiming, within a family and historical context, his own self from a terrifying period without that self. This added layer of meaning only increases the power of this work and my admiration for this artist. I now understand the clarity of conviction with which he spoke in our Grand Hall in front of hundreds of strangers; he knew what it was like to lose everything, and somehow he had emerged on a quest without any visible remnants of fear.

What if we, as a region and society, could learn from this artist about the power of releasing the taught versions of our selves and our social structures to the point that what remains is only the courage of honesty and the will to make, through beauty and imagery and imagination, things whole in a reconstructed life? Noah's epic painting, although based on a factual framework, does not contain all of the facts. But it does contain the truth.

This project at the Mississippi Museum of Art (MMA) would not be possible without Noah's trust and partnership, and his companions along the way, namely Stephen Parks and the investigators at the Asylum Hill Research Consortium led by Lida Gibson and Dr. Ralph Didlake. At MMA, the exhibition was guided by the capable hand of curator Dr. Megan Hines, our Mellon postdoctoral fellow from 2021 to 2023. She and her colleagues Lydia Jasper, Grayston Barron, Kathleen Barnett,

Sarah Wade, Kaegan Sparks, Elisabeth Callihan, and Daleicia Hart became part of Noah's band of journey folk along the way. Also at MMA, Jana Brady and Andrea Donelson led the exhibition's marketing efforts to ensure that Noah's vision is experienced by our entire community. The thoughtful exhibition design has been beautifully rendered by Robin Dietrick of Symmetry LLC, our consistent and award-winning partner. The catalogue is strengthened by the words and questions of Noah's friend Ann Patchett, the design of Karen Cronin, and the scholarship of Drs. Amy Forbes and Patrick Hopkins, and Timothy Hyman. We're grateful to Millsaps College for our academic partnership that includes sharing students and scholars, and—in this case—space for a "test run" of the exhibition. Finally, the Institute of Museum and Library Services provided a generous grant to support the development of the exhibition and the National Archives Digitization Program supported its public programming. Without these partners and individuals, we would not be able to share this magnificent work.

Betsy Bradley
Laurie Hearin McRee Director
Mississippi Museum of Art

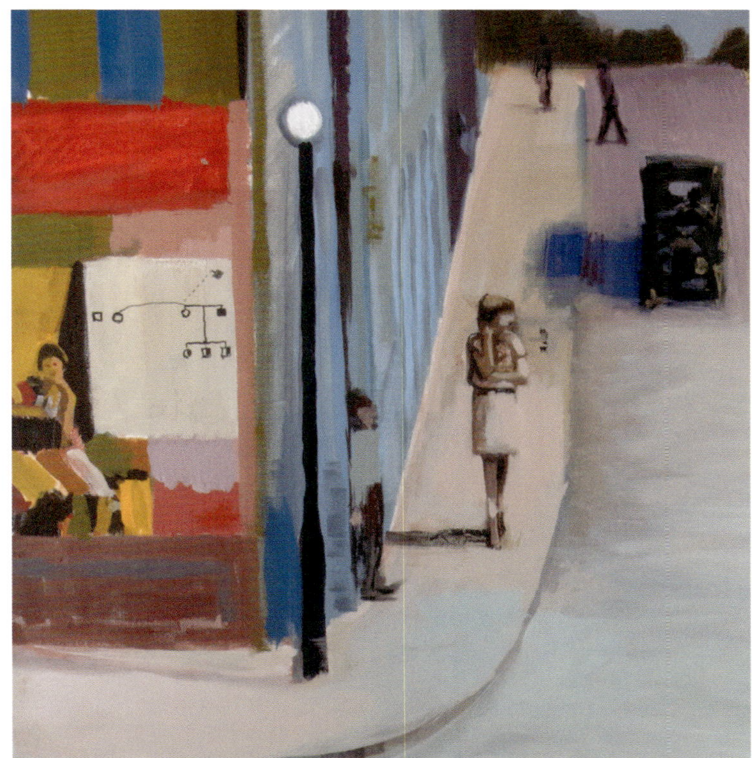

INTRODUCTION

MEGAN HINES, PHD

NOAH SATERSTROM'S PAINTING *What Became of Dr. Smith* (2023) is his most ambitious project to date in both form and content. Yet, despite its leap forward into new territory, it represents a remarkably logical progression in his career, which has produced thousands of paintings narrativizing his family's stories and Southern histories. At six feet tall and 122 feet in length, the painting is made up of 183 canvases hung together in a grid. It is a panoramic visual narrative of the life of Dr. David Lawson (D.L.) Lemmon Smith (1891–1965), Saterstrom's great-grandfather. Erased from the family record, Dr. Smith was a mysterious figure lurking in Saterstrom's past, conspicuous in his absence. Saterstrom's well-documented family history, with roots in Mississippi dating to the late eighteenth century, has served as a deep well from which he draws stories and images for his painting practice. In his work, the stories of his well-off white family intertwine with Mississippi's far, middle, and recent pasts. This inheritance serves as neither burden nor blessing for Saterstrom. Rather, it is like the surface of a trampoline. By varying his approach, he can project himself in different directions. Like the long history of painting itself, Saterstrom's family's stories, and Mississippi's stories, offer many ways forward.

The history of Dr. Smith had been excised from Saterstrom's heritage, but through the artist's research and interpretation, his great-grandfather has been reinserted into the family story. That narrative is woven across the 732 square feet of the painting and told in various forms in the texts included in this catalogue. But in short, it is this: Dr. Smith, an optometrist, had a mental break in his thirties. Experiencing delusions and accused of rape, he was hospitalized and spent the last forty years of his life in the Mississippi State Hospital in Jackson, later located at Whitfield. His wife and four children lived on, and eventually Dr. Smith became a distant memory, nearly forgotten, even while he still lived. Once Saterstrom had gathered enough of these facts of his life to create a cohesive narrative, the question remained: how to depict it?

Saterstrom's family story and Southern heritage are not his only inheritance. As a painter, he is a recipient of an art historical legacy. The crux of Dr. Smith's story is the transformation of his life due to mental illness. Numerous tropes related to mental illness exist within the Western painting tradition that Saterstrom could have relied on to convey this pivotal part of his story. Many have been in circulation since the Renaissance, yet it was during the European Enlightenment,

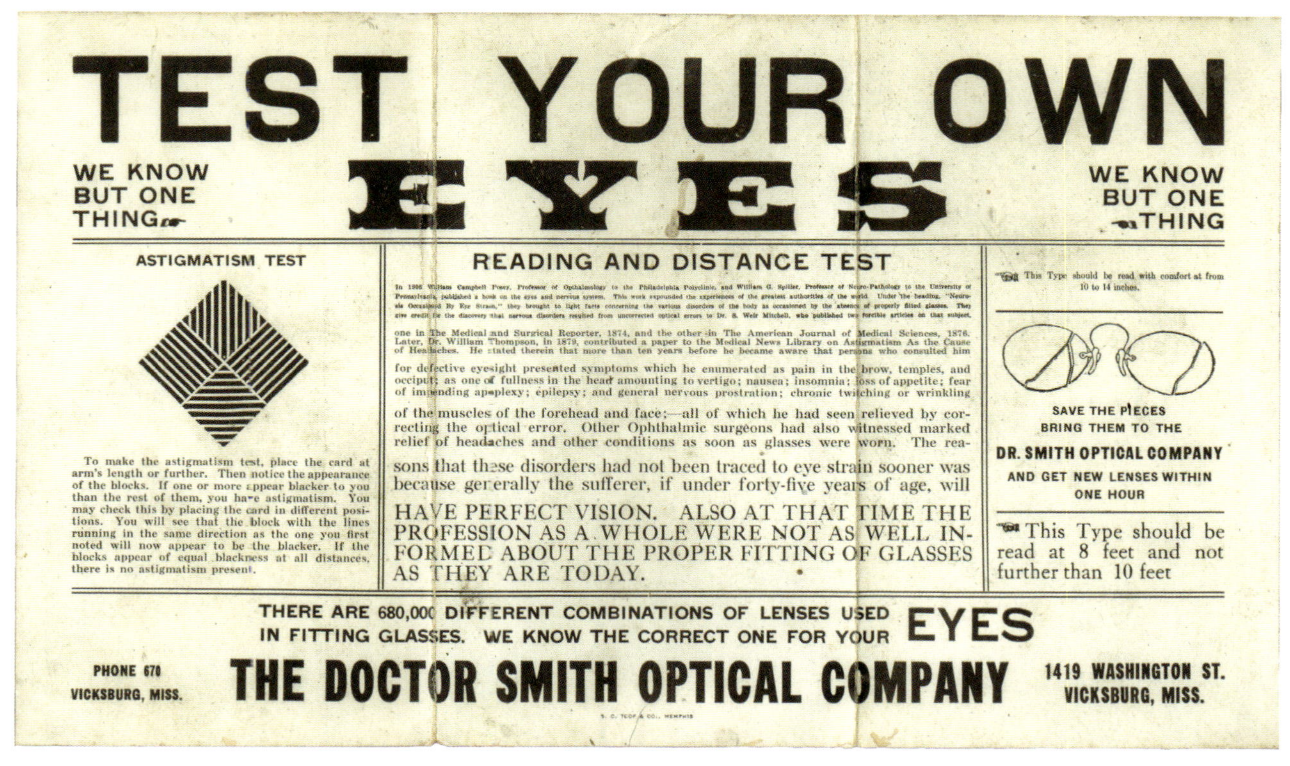

A poster advertising the Doctor Smith Optical Company in Vicksburg, Mississippi, ca. 1919.

when art became a tool of visual diagnosis, that standardized images of what mental illness "looks like" began to take shape.[1] From this period emerged images of the "raving madman," a combination of earlier understandings of people with mental illness as wild and animal-like with Enlightenment-era visualizations of physiognomic types.[2] As a figurative painter, Saterstrom could have employed these ingrained tropes. However, those images from the past are notably absent from *What Became of Dr. Smith*. Saterstrom chose to invent his own images rather than reproduce the established visual codes of mental illness.

The idea that art is a creative act, capable of making visible what would otherwise go unnoticed, or perhaps be impossible to see at all, was established by the early twentieth-century Modernists. Artist

Paul Klee stated, "Art does not reproduce the visible; rather it makes visible."[3] This shift in focus, from reproduction to production, opened new avenues for painting, including experimentation with expression and abstraction. In *What Became of Dr. Smith*, Saterstrom adopts this approach to make apparent Dr. Smith's indelible and unique place in the world. Painting Dr. Smith's story from birth to death is a productive action by Saterstrom, one which not only inserts his narrative into history, but transforms viewers' existing notions of who is part of history. To emphasize the transformative power of painting, the artist foregrounds his work within the painting itself, depicting himself at an easel twice within the central space dedicated to Dr. Smith's major transformation. Saterstrom's painting, like Dr. Smith's work as an optometrist, aims to sharpen our vision. In *What Became of Dr. Smith*, not only do we see a man who was erased due to the taboo of mental illness; we also are challenged to see individuality and complexity in place of stereotypes.

The essays in this catalogue delve into the personal and shared histories that inform *What Became of Dr. Smith*. Saterstrom's statement discloses the personal revelation provoked by the process of researching and painting Dr. Smith's life. Author and friend of the artist Ann Patchett interviews Saterstrom, who discusses this project in relation to his development as an artist. Artist, mentor, and friend Timothy Hyman relates *What Became of Dr. Smith* to a long history of narrative painting, going back to fourteenth-century Italian frescoes. Drs. Amy Forbes and Patrick Hopkins provide a historical account of the Mississippi State Lunatic Asylum, later named the State Insane Hospital, from its opening in 1855 to its closing in 1935. Finally, a chronology of Dr. Smith's life consolidates the six years of research that Saterstrom has completed thus far on the life of his great-grandfather. ■

[1] Sander L. Gilman, *Seeing the Insane: A Visual and Cultural History of Our Attitudes Toward the Mentally Ill* (Brattleboro, VT: Echo Point Books & Media, 2014).

[2] Gilman, "The Medical Illustration of Madness," in *Seeing the Insane*, 72–101.

[3] Paul Klee, "Creative Confession, 1920," in *Creative Confession and Other Writings*, ed. Matthew Gale (London: Tate Publishing, 2013), 7.

Noah Saterstrom, What Became of Dr. Smith *(detail), 2023.*

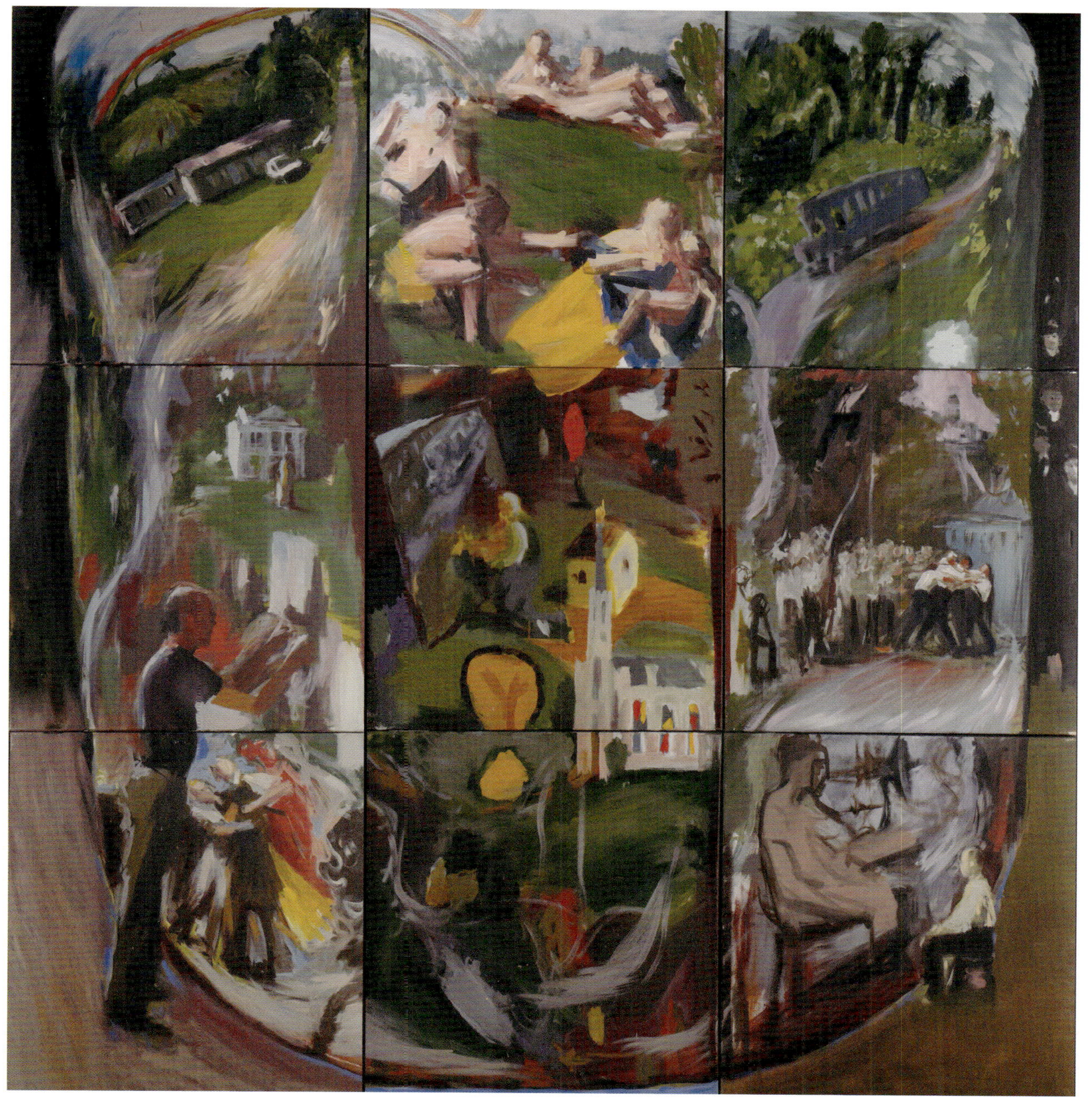

WHAT BECAME OF DR. SMITH

NOAH SATERSTROM

IN 1915, TWENTY-FOUR-YEAR-OLD David Lawson (D.L.) Lemmon Smith arrived in Natchez, Mississippi, and established the Dr. Smith Optical Company office on Main Street. Less than a decade later, his life had grown to include a wife, four children, a traveling optometry truck, a host of delusions, an assault charge, and an involuntary committal to the Mississippi State Insane Hospital. The rest of his days were spent in confinement, and Dr. Smith, my great-grandfather, died a resident of the Mississippi State Hospital at Whitfield some forty years later. We think his body, unclaimed by his descendants, was buried on the hospital grounds. Perhaps it was, but there is so much we don't know. Dr. Smith was nearly erased from my—our—family's history, made a ghost by the peculiar combination of shame and pride that weaves its way through so many ancestral tales of the Deep South. His is a story, gothic and dark, plucked from Faulkner. But that's not why I painted it.

In the summer of 1999 I moved to Glasgow, Scotland, also twenty-four years old, and by that October was newly married, well into my first semester of art school, and living in a freezing, damp flat on a narrow street in the West End. Within two years I was back in the US, divorced, and in the midst of an episode of depersonalization so intense I became convinced that not only did I not exist, but I had never existed. My memories were not my own, my voice was that of another, my hands felt barely connected to my wrists. I stopped painting, I went to therapy, and I breathed rhythmically. I tried everything to feel like anything but a ghost.

It took me years to drag myself from the depths of dissociation into the semblance of real life. What eventually pulled me back from the existential abyss was painting scenes from my old family photograph albums. We have a lot of family photographs. Our albums are arranged by year and each one holds images of presents being unwrapped, family gatherings, dinners, road trips—the cycle of each year. Here in 1910, David's wife, Ethel, sits with her school friends, laughing hysterically at a joke long gone. There in 1920, young Margaret, Ethel and David's daughter and my grandmother, stands in a neatly pressed pinafore sewn by her grandmother. Here in 1946, my mother in a highchair holds a silver cup, one I still know, as light streams across her face, one I already recognize as my mother's. There in 1980, my sister and I are playing Sorry on a green shag rug. Here is my head, freshly bandaged from a car accident the summer after my fourth grade year, taken the afternoon I got the scar I see in the mirror every day.

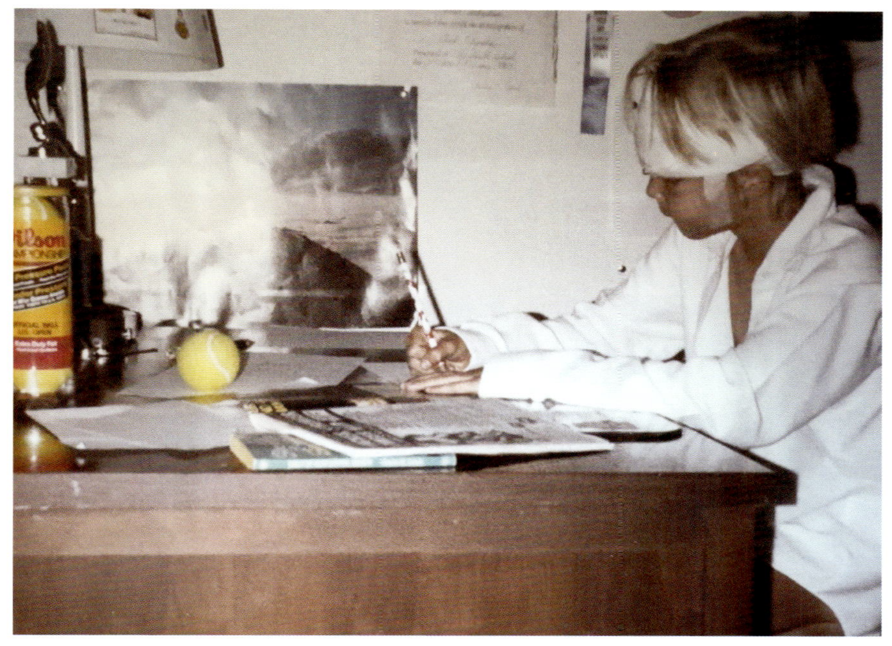

Noah Saterstrom as a child, summer 1984.

I painted as many of the photographs as I could. I painted them not only because I thought they'd make good paintings, but because when I studied them, my memories became mine again. This was the dream of time travel made real. As I looked closely at the light on my grandmother's face as she waved us off from her front steps, I felt the seatbelt across my small body and the heat of the buckle. I could smell the earth under the nearby live oaks and hear her voice, "Toodle-loo," as we drove away.

Desperately holding on to the first sense of self I'd had in years, I found myself wanting to stare into each image for hours. Painting gave me permission to do that. I could take one photograph, a record of a millisecond, and study its details for hours, a whole day. This was how my memories came back to me and how I came to love painting again. The further I got from my years of dissociation, the easier it became to forget I'd ever lost myself at all. I didn't paint Dr. Smith then, either. He was still a ghost, even if I wasn't. Anymore.

Eventually, I married again, had three kids, and began to enjoy some success as a painter. In the mid-2010s I started work on my biggest (physically and figuratively) piece to date: *Road to Shubuta* (2016), the visual story of my ancestors' Civil War–era flight from Natchez. Enslavers, they escaped east in an attempt to evade the Union occupation. The painting was acquired by the Mississippi Museum of Art and featured in their exhibition *Picturing Mississippi, 1817–2017: Land of Plenty, Pain, and Promise*. Thoughts of Dr. Smith popped up from time to time, and while in Jackson for the show's opening, I went to the Mississippi Department of Archives and History to see what I could learn about my great-grandfather. There in a dusty leather-bound ledger with "Mississippi Insane Hospital" on the spine was his name in faded black ink: "Dr. David Lemmon

Smith, Claiborne County." The other columns were left blank—no cause for committal, no next of kin, no diagnosis, no release date.

Twenty years before visiting the archives and tumbling down the rabbit hole of research into Smith's life, I was sitting with Margaret while we looked at a family album in her library. Then in her nineties, Grandmother still kept a small photograph of her father on her desk, more than eighty years since his disappearance, though I never heard her mention him. In one photo, baby Margaret sits on the hood of a Model T and a man's hand reaches out to stabilize her. I said, "Is that your father's hand?" She nodded. "What can you tell me about him?" She answered, tightly, "He was an optometrist." She paused as we both waited for more words. None came. Instead, she told me about the azaleas in her grandmother's garden, how beautiful they were. I nodded and asked no more questions. We turned the page.

Decades later, turning the page of the Old Asylum ledger and seeing my great-grandfather's name opened up a well of questions I could no longer dismiss, and I felt a new sense of urgency around my research. With the help of Stephen Parks, the state librarian, I pieced together a detailed picture of Dr. Smith's life before his hospitalization. The story that unfolded was cinematic in scope. But while I'd gone into the task not expecting to like everything I learned (a speculation that's proven true), what I did not anticipate was that Dr. Smith's story would be as much a lens through which to see my own experience of mental illness as it is a generations-removed tale of a man locked away for life.

As I read Dr. Smith's correspondence and combed through unearthed articles about his travels and flights of fancy, the picture that emerged was one of a certainly ill man. Years of research turned up more and more detail, and I found myself thinking with near obsession about Dr. Smith. The closer I came to piecing together the mystery of his life, the more I identified with him. It became impossible to work on anything else until I painted his life and did my best to capture as much of his story as I could. Painting everything I found about Dr. Smith became a way for me to try to understand why I made it through, but he remained lost.

The life Dr. Smith planned for himself was derailed by mental illness and, as a result, he was removed from his family and society. Like his, my connection to reality was strained and eventually severed by stressful life events, but that's where our stories diverge. Somehow, I rebuilt myself. I didn't disappear. What about him? Did he suffer the full forty years he was in state custody? Did he undergo painful treatments? Was he subject to inhumane conditions, or was he treated kindly and fairly? According to sparse family rumors, he was offered release multiple times, but refused. Did he recover as I did, but had no life to return to?

Dr. Smith was allegedly part of the groundskeeping crew at the Mississippi State Hospital at Whitfield. There's some evidence he may even have employed his skills as an optometrist for fellow residents. A newspaper article shows him weaving in the occupational therapy program. Did he have friends? Did he love? Was he happy? Whatever the circumstances, more than half of his seventy-four years were lived after he "disappeared." Even if the records of his stay are eventually uncovered, there is no way we will ever know all the answers. They're gone. When I lost myself, painting my family's past built a ladder out of the well into which I had fallen. Maybe this painting of Dr. Smith's life is my attempt to throw his memory a rope.

My intention was to figure out what happened to my great-grandfather, not to resurrect my own experience. Frankly, it's something I have spent decades trying to forget. The idea that any of us at any moment could be overtaken by a mental disorder can effectively keep us from talking about it at all, afraid we will pull the darkness to us. But the artistic process has a way of driving us toward honesty and openness. When I realized that in painting Dr. Smith's story I was partly painting my own, it became harder to avoid my own experience of delusions and dissociation.

Art cannot right the wrongs of history or make a malfunctioning mind whole. The past is gone except inasmuch as we call a version of it into our stories and pictures. What art can do is remind us that every moment is valuable, even the unbearable ones, and every moment is worthy of note, even the mundane ones. It is the accumulation of these extraordinary instances and ordinary days that make us human and give contour to our lives. In accepting that Dr. Smith's mind and mine bear more than a passing resemblance, I am certain that Dr. Smith had his share of the unbearable and the mundane. Like me, he existed both as an absence and a presence, whether or not he was allowed the privilege of doing so in the public eye. The title of this painting, *What Became of Dr. Smith*, is not the question I first asked, but a simple statement of fact. It is a surrogate for the man who was erased, and an alternative to generations of silence. This painting is what became of Dr. Smith. ■

WHAT BECAME OF DR. SMITH

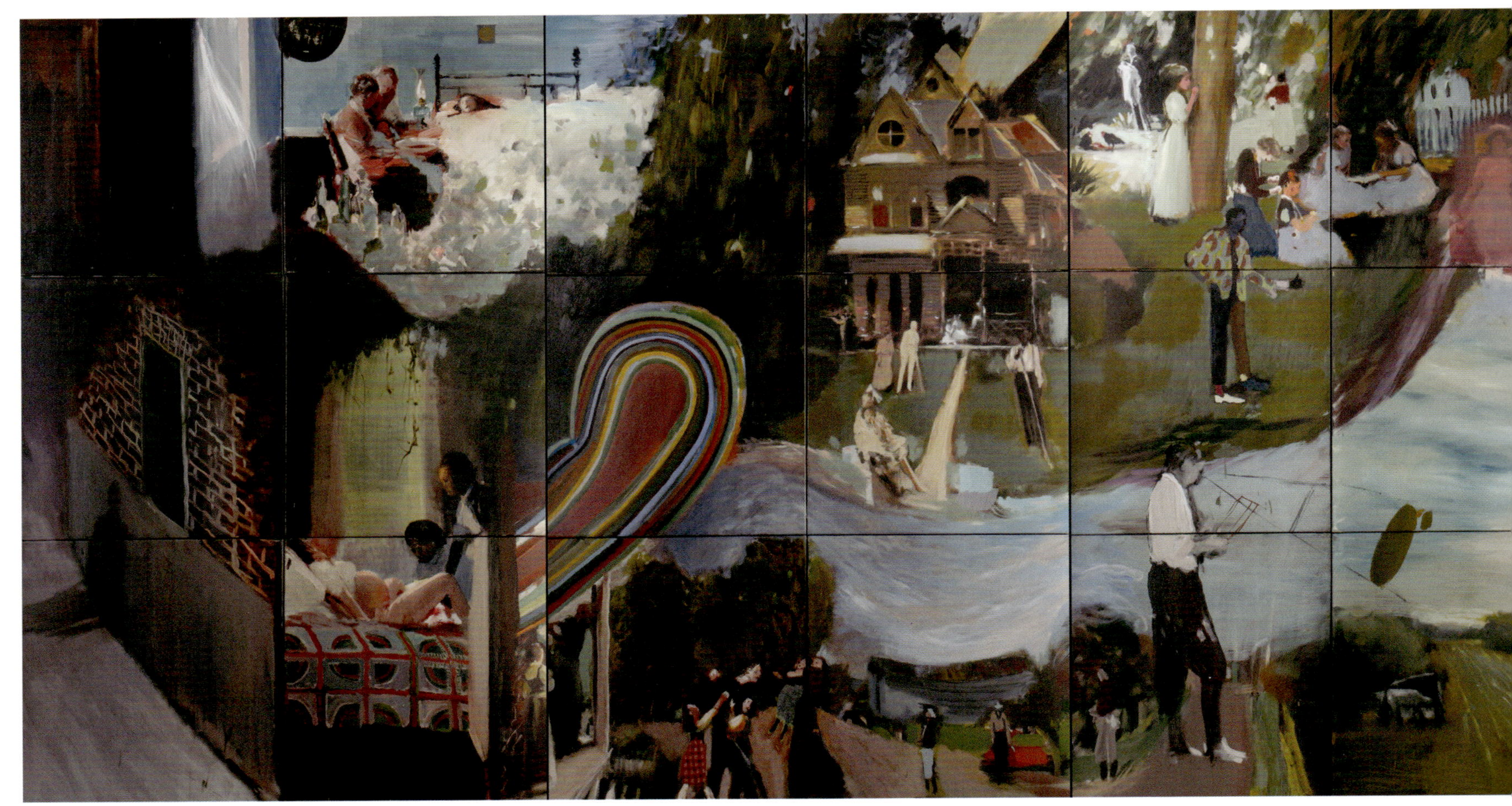

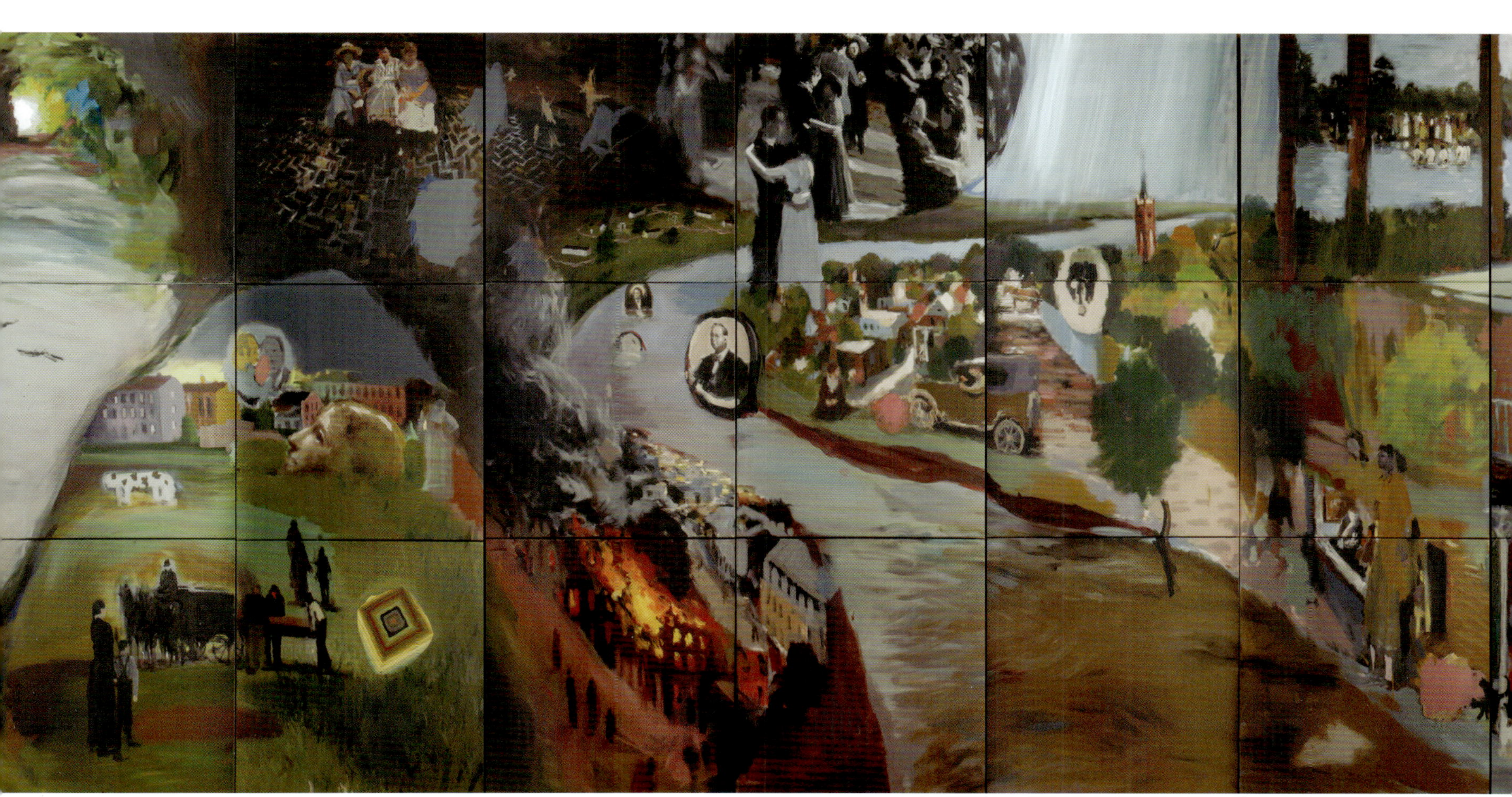

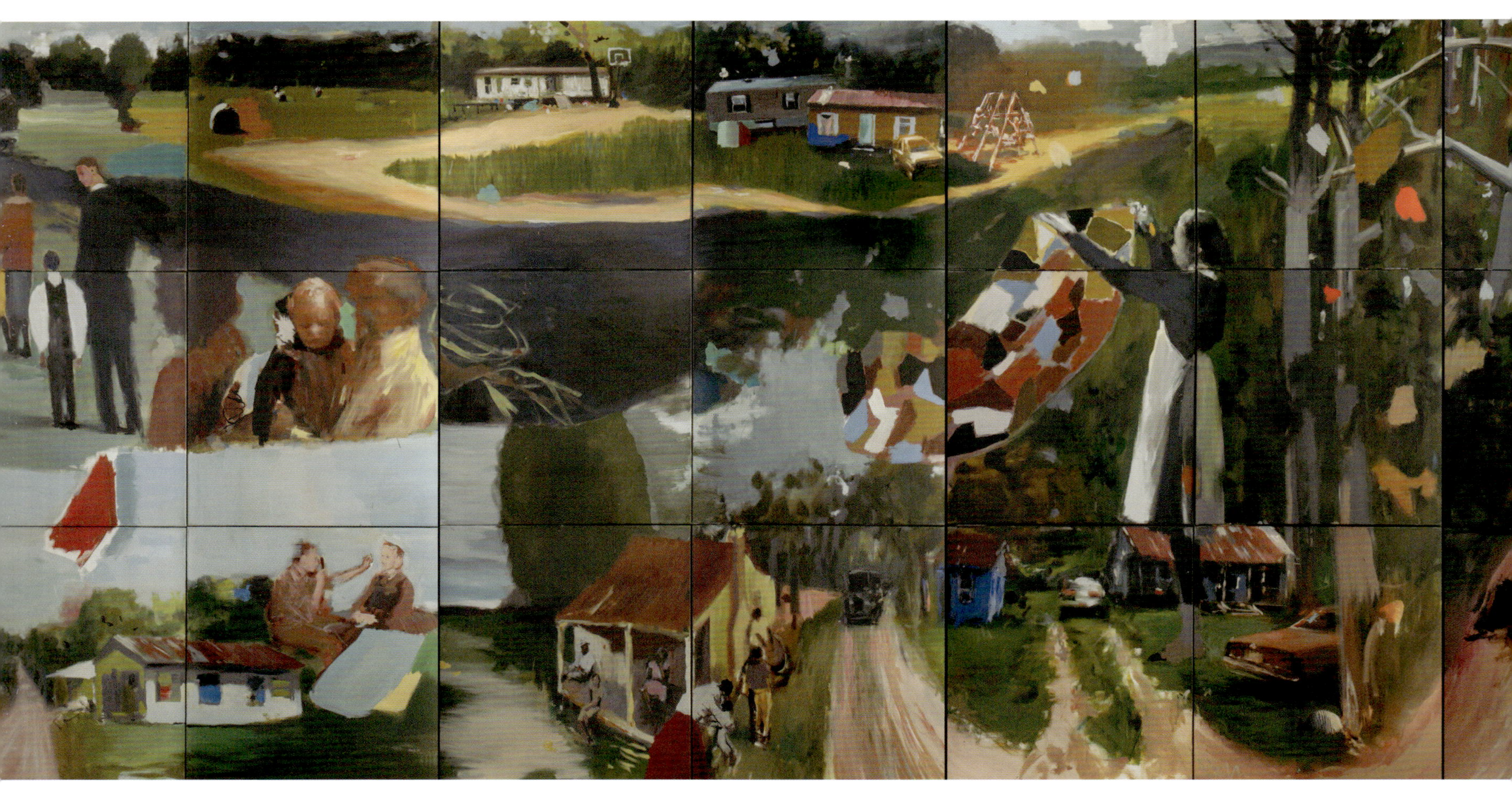

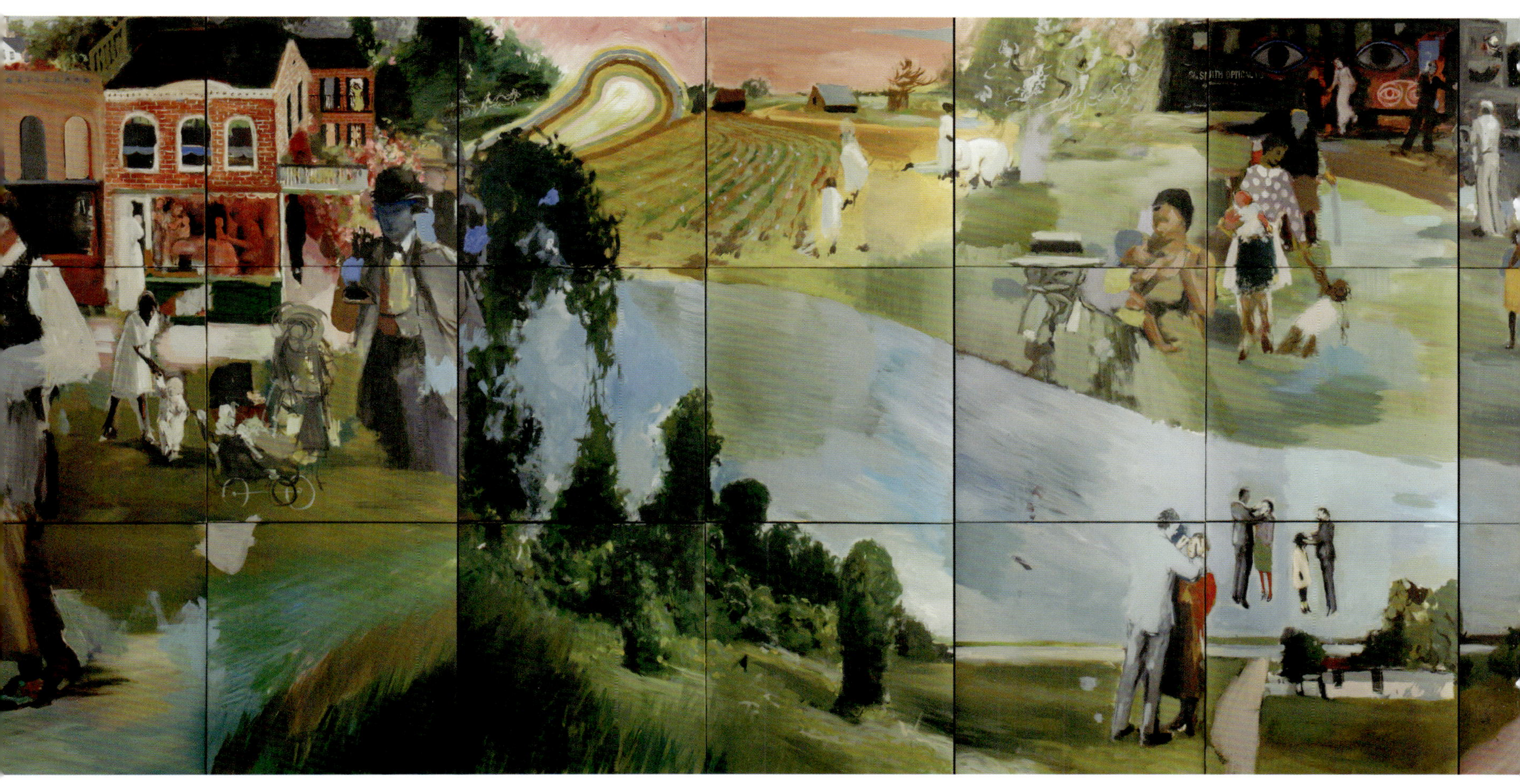
SMITH OPTICAL

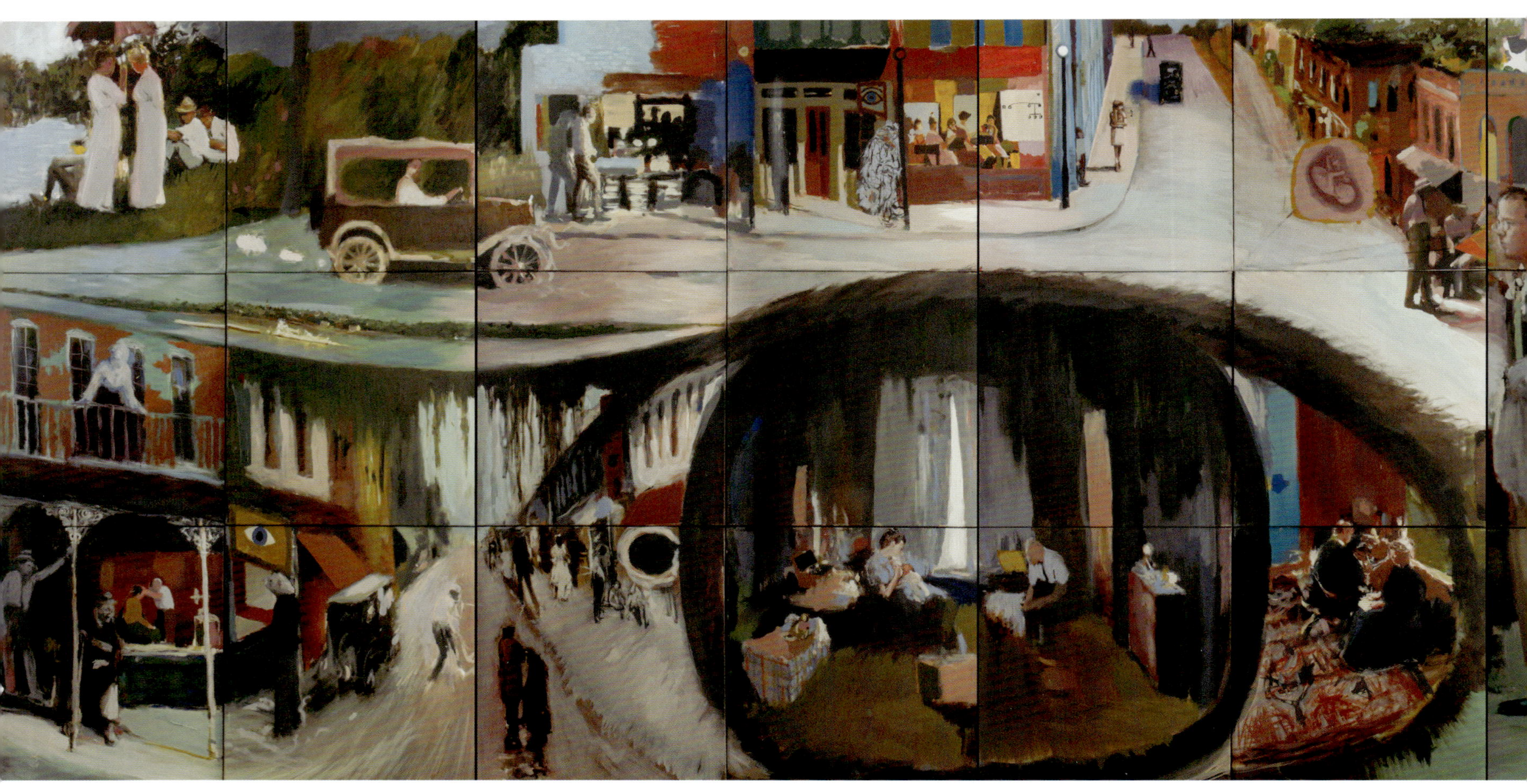

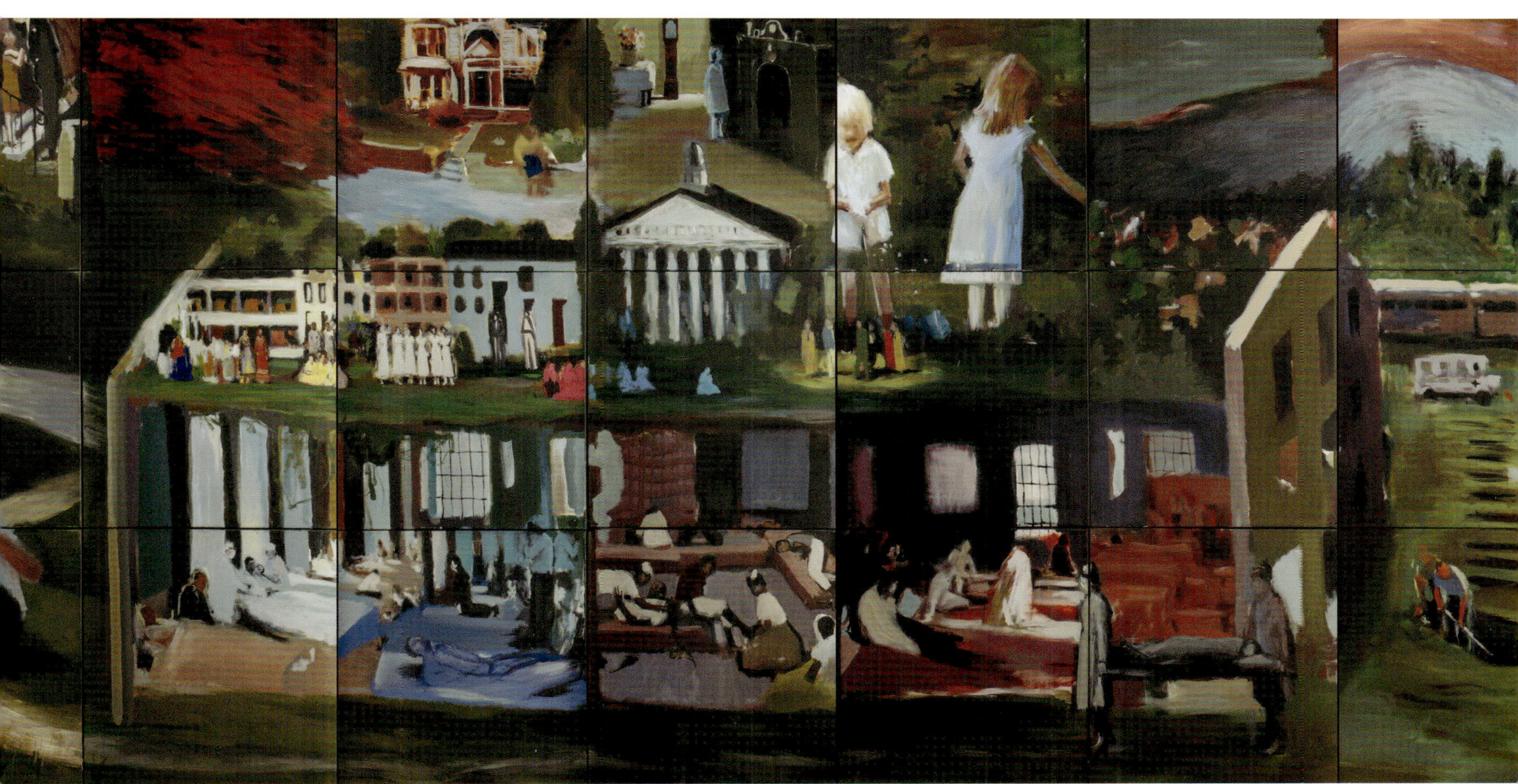

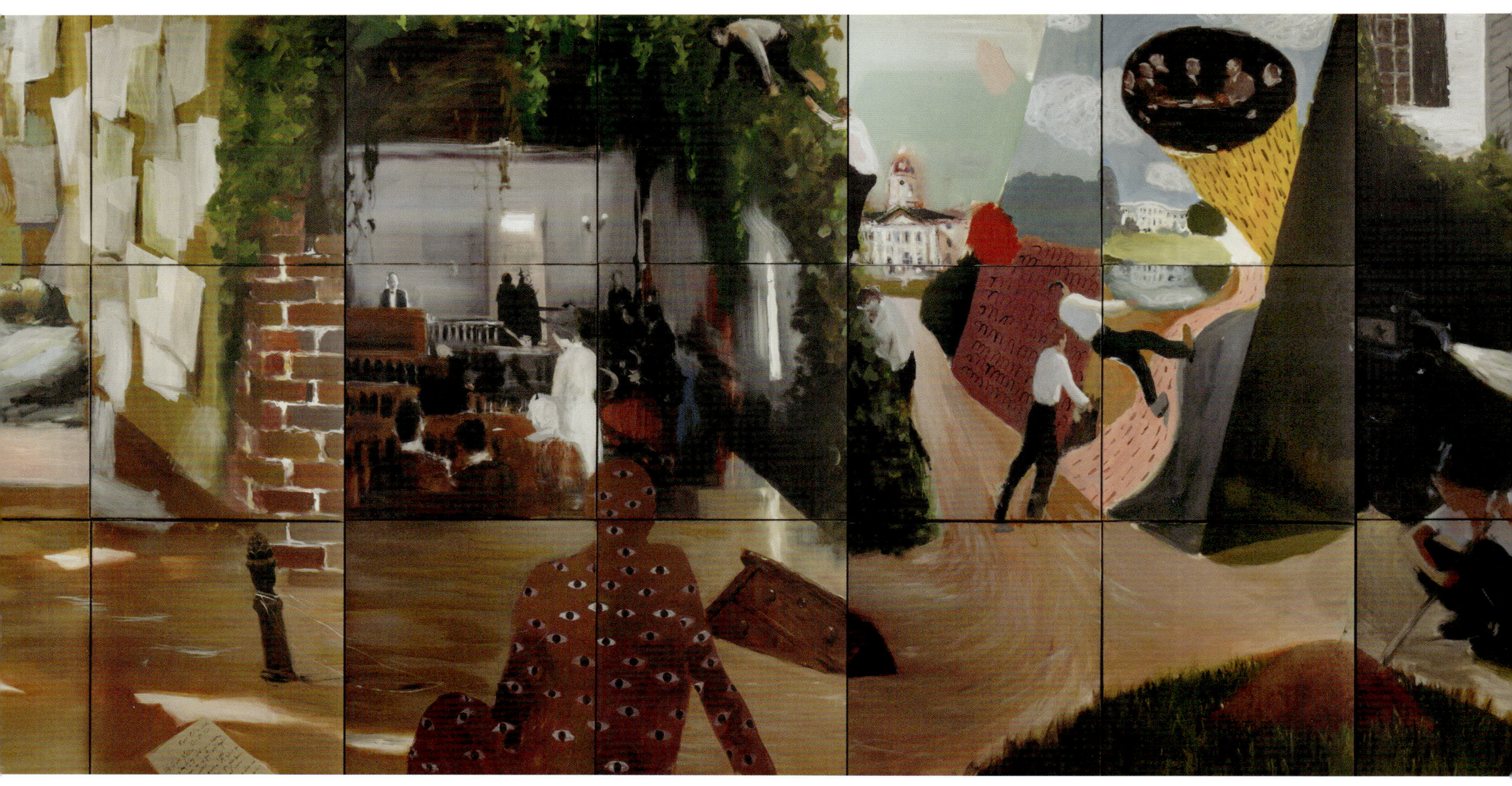

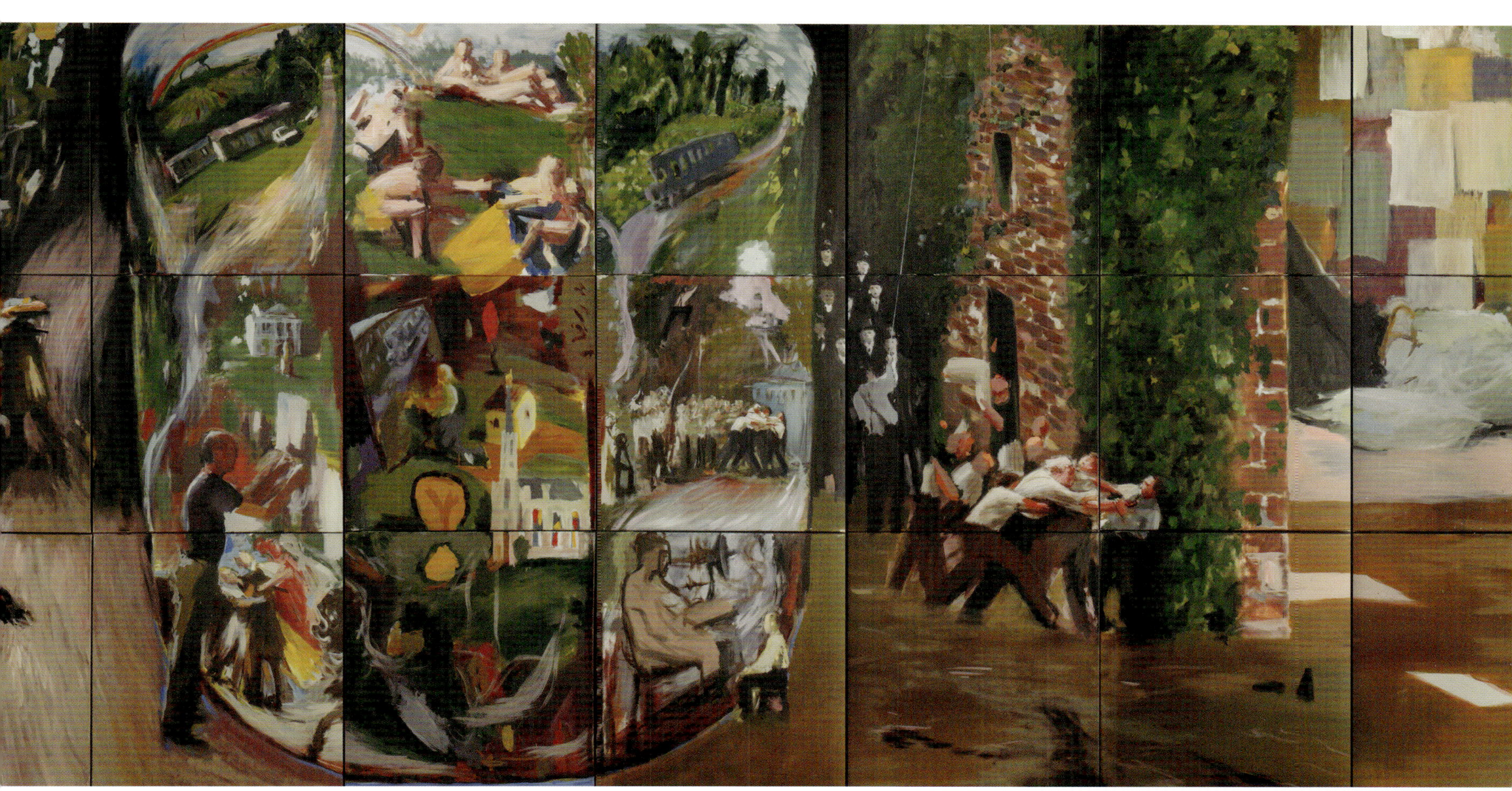

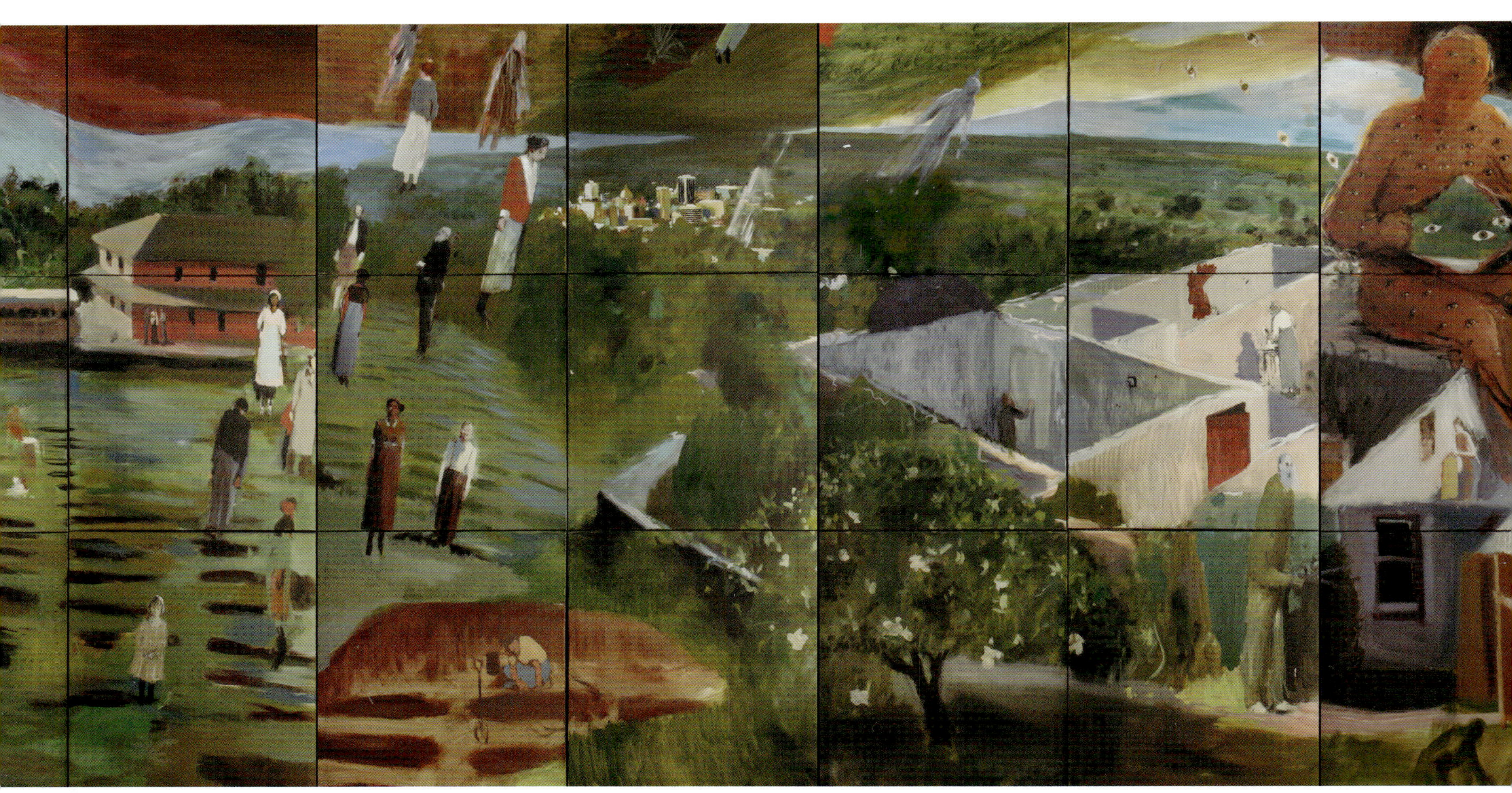

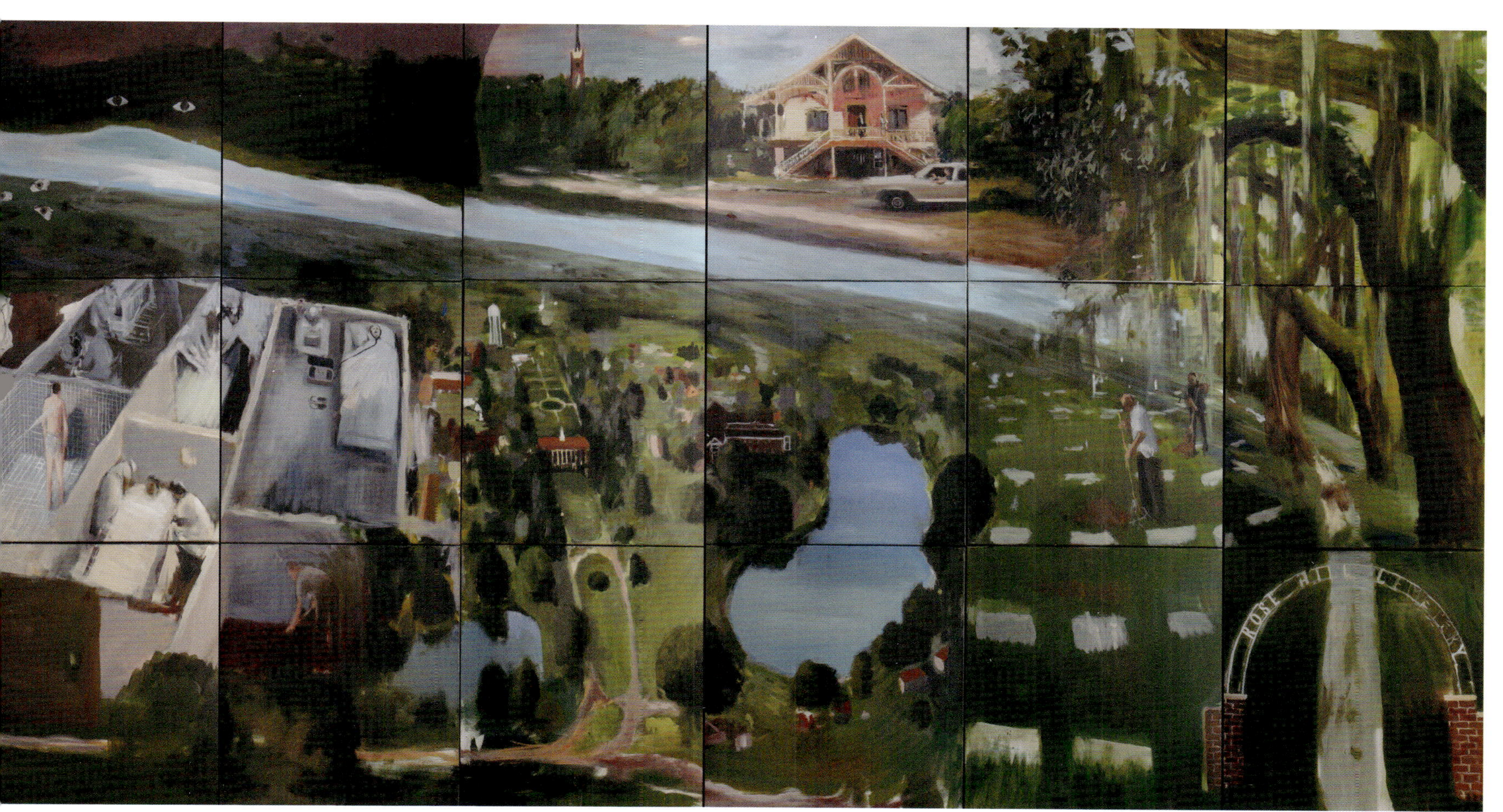
ROSE

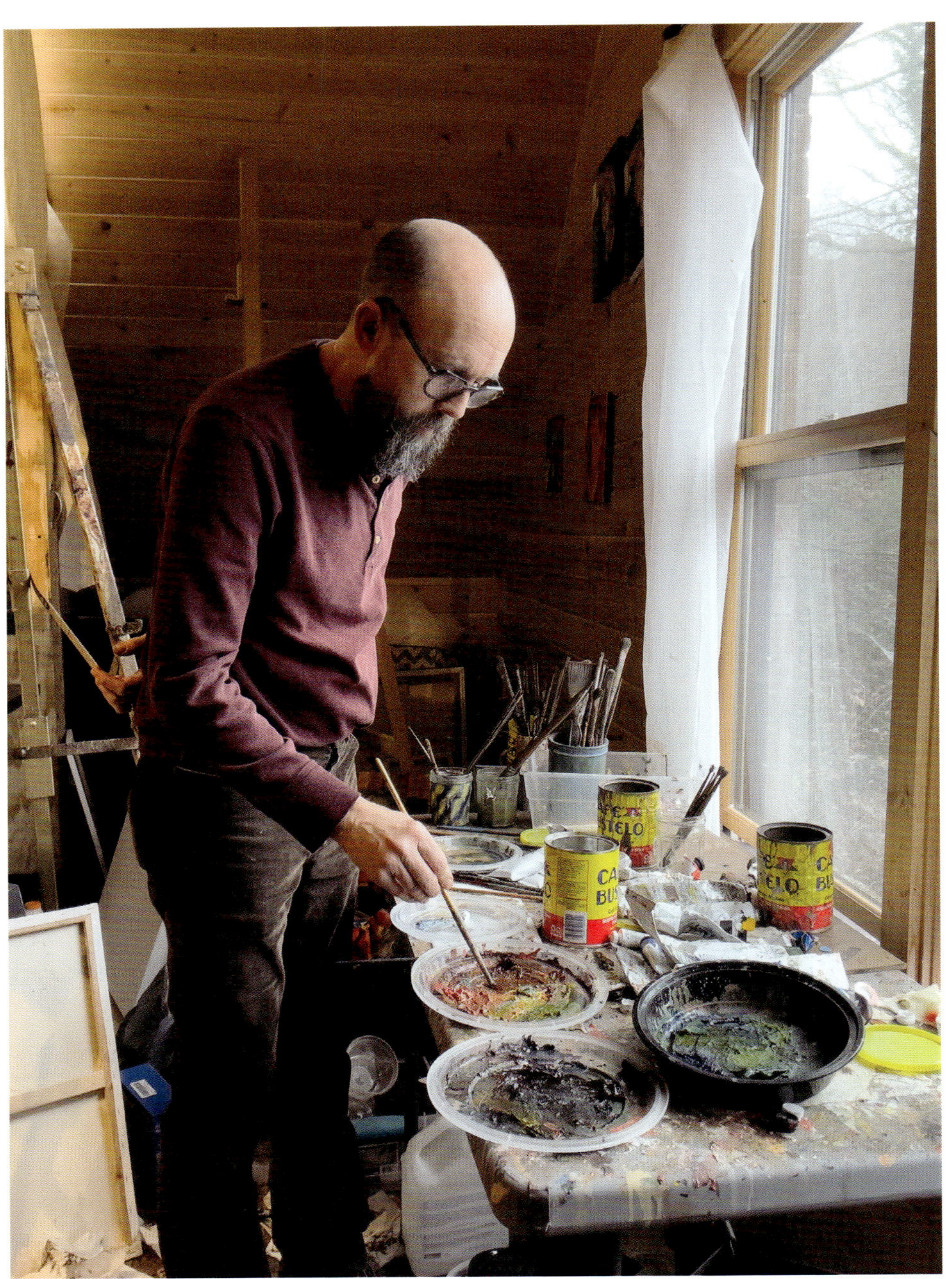

Noah Saterstrom in his studio, 2023.

NOAH SATERSTROM AND ANN PATCHETT IN CONVERSATION

IDEAS DON'T GET MUCH BIGGER than Noah Saterstrom's painting that traces the life of his great-grandfather, Dr. Smith. The physical piece is comprised of 183 canvases, each two feet square, hung together in a grid of three rows that stretches 122 feet wide. The emotional scope covers family history and Southern history seen through the lens of mental illness. The result is magnificent, urgent, disquieting. Be it by water or smoke or the turning of roads across the canvases, the viewer is carried deep into the narrative. To consider this work strictly in terms of color, movement, and execution is to be deeply satisfied, but to understand what is unfolding is to appreciate it at another level. Sitting in Noah's studio in Nashville as he put up twenty-four canvases at a time, I felt like I was walking into a novel playing out as a painting. It made perfect sense. He and I have been talking about this project for years, two friends having breakfast, but to see it was something else entirely. This is our conversation.

AP: Start at the beginning, please.

NS: We moved around a lot when I was a child because my father was transferred for insurance sales work: Vermont, Massachusetts, Natchez, Shreveport, Wisconsin, back to Shreveport. We came to Natchez again when I was eleven and stayed there until I was through high school. I very much think of myself as a Mississippian. Natchez was, and I suppose still is, "home." It's beautiful and hideous and has affected me in ways I will never understand, no matter how much I paint and blather on about it.

AP: What was your early exposure to art?

NS: I began drawing pretty constantly as a child. I remember people referring to me as an artist, or "an artistic type" (which isn't always a compliment) from my early teen years. No one seemed to anticipate me doing anything else, at least that's my impression. The art I was exposed to was mostly of the homey and uplifting variety: Norman Rockwell, Carl Larsson, Mary Cassatt, and lots of children's book illustrations, Wallace Tripp.

AP: That's a good lineup for childhood, comforting and stable. Rockwell gives a sense of narrative. Cassatt and Larsson provide a sympathy for beauty. I think about the portrait you painted for the cover of my book *The Dutch House*. There's some Cassatt in there. What's your relationship to beauty?

NS: I think *The Dutch House* cover works because Maeve [the main character] is disquieting as well as beautiful; the two are fused. I spent endless hours as a little kid tracing from a huge Rockwell book at my grandparents' house. I loved the competence, the story. There was a stack of paper with "Great American Reserve" letterhead and I drew and drew and drew. When I was old enough to research art, I bent toward edgier things. I was drawn to medieval painting and sculptures which were upsetting but not repellent. I was raised Catholic and the font of that imagery has been foundational. When I first started teaching myself to draw and paint as a teenager, I would go to the Natchez library and my Aunt Kathy, the librarian, fed me books of Dürer, Donatello, the Sistine Chapel, and I would draw from the pictures. I loved the mythic narratives. Strange and violent images with odd contortions of time and space took a while to work its way into my work, but I see it now. You'll have an Annunciation with the Archangel Michael announcing to Mary that her son will be born, and standing behind Michael may be St. Dominic with a sword through his head for having been killed for his devotion to the baby who is being announced. All in one image. That kind of layering fascinates me and this big painting starts out with a similar folding of time.

AP: Did you have an idea of what an "artist's life" would look like when you were a child?

NS: Yes, I could wear a tunic and live in Italy.

AP: I was going to live in a garret in Paris and write by the light of a candle stub. We could have hung out together.

NS: I doubt we would have met; I was going to fourteenth-century Italy.

AP: But then you went to college instead.

NS: The University of Mississippi. Not a great student, just wanted to paint. My painting professor more or less just let me do that, for which I was grateful, though I could have used more guidance. I didn't learn much in the way of material handling and technical painting (which explains my horrid brush and palette habits). When I got to Scotland for graduate school, I had a horrible deficit. Disgraceful, truly. I had felt in Mississippi that painting was a fringe activity because there was little context, then got to art school and discovered it was a fringe activity for an opposite reason. Everyone was doing installation, video, text interventions, conceptual work, and performances. I was disoriented and adrift. The undergrad students had a more traditional education. The MFA program was all self-directed studio work and critiques. As I remember it, when I joined in the late nineties, there were forty students and I was the only painter. Times have changed a lot since then; narrative painting is perfectly acceptable now in a way it wasn't then. There was lots of vitriol. Cheeky, self-referential concept work had eclipsed painting. I felt like a cobbler or wheelwright or something. I went to a talk by Timothy Hyman who had written a book on Bonnard, whom I loved. I introduced myself and he came to my studio the next day and stayed for hours. He was appalled at how little I knew. He wrote page after page of names of painters I needed to study and form opinions about. He actually said to me, "What did you used to do?" which was embarrassing because art was all I had ever done. I have considered Tim a kind of mentor ever since. Those years of thinking about and talking about painting have been invaluable. Tim's relentless criticism and encouragement has been my single biggest influence, especially regarding figuration and narrative.

AP: And where did figuration and narrative take you?

NS: I loved the Impressionists and elegant portraitists like Sargent. The Renaissance was too muscular for me, but copying those images helped me learn technique, light/dark, harmonic composition, etc. It wasn't until I got to graduate school in Scotland that I really dunked myself in work that was long established in the canon: Francis Bacon, Balthus, Guston. Beautiful but also violent, vile, unsettling. I struggled to reconcile my love of beautiful painting with a new mistrust of beautiful painting. Now it's just a lifelong question—a good thing. I went deeper into more contemporary work: Nicole Eisenman, Dana Schutz, Ken Kiff, R.B. Kitaj, Larry Rivers, Francesco Clemente, Leon Golub, Susan Rothenberg, Bhupen Khakhar. I didn't have much interest in Abstract Expressionism. I wanted to make pictures and resented the obsession with pure form, object, and performance, a self-protective resentment that I've gotten over.

Anyway, beauty, yes, I think it has an important role in *confronting* difficult things. Not in avoiding difficult things. It's easier to look at a beautiful painting of something hard, than a repellent image of something hard, right?

AP: Which leads us nicely to Dr. Smith. At what point did you first become aware of him? When did you start to realize this story was important to you?

NS: According to my mother, I've been interested in the story (or lack of) since I first heard of him as a kid. My mother had only some family rumors to go on. She had looked through microfiche and newspaper clippings trying to put together her grandfather's history and came up with nothing. In high school and college, I would occasionally ask my grandmother questions about her father, but she couldn't get through a sentence about him being an optometrist without seizing up. She had a photo of Dr. Smith on her desk when she died, ninety years after his disappearance. That seething silence is crushing to me. To think that if I disappeared today, my daughter, Vivian, could have a photo of me on her desk in the year . . . 2112? And unable to say more than "he was a painter." How devastating is that? When the family was moving

Grandmother to assisted living in 2006, I was digging through a secret passageway on the third floor of her family home—boxes of ancestral linens and undergarments, half-digested by squirrels and mice—and found Dr. Smith's traveling optometry kit. I couldn't bring myself to open it until about 2017 when I started this whole thing in earnest.

AP: How much of Dr. Smith's story is you wrestling with your own legacy as a Southerner?

NS: Hard to say if it's wrestling with being a Southerner, or as a self-employed father of a bunch of kids. Or someone devoted to seeing. I have a deep fear of mental illness and had a notable extended episode of delusions in my early twenties that terrified and reshaped me.

AP: Do you want to tell me about it?

NS: Not something I've talked much about, but I guess I need to for this show. In 2001, I had a significant breakdown. Years of isolation, dissolution of a troubled marriage, too much time painting, poor health, too much Scottish rain, all of the above? I lost my sense of self. Like—utterly. To say it was an identity crisis doesn't capture it. I lost my memories. My history had been erased and replaced by an exact replica. Nothing could convince me otherwise. I'd go to sleep and wake back up into the same nightmare. I didn't see any way forward but to be institutionalized for life and was just waiting for everyone else to figure that out. But at some point I found photo albums from my childhood and started painting those pictures one after another. By doing that, I remembered how much I loved painting, and gradually started to believe that it didn't matter if my memories were real. I don't know how long this lasted, maybe a year, but since I emerged there's never been a hint of recurrence. Had I known as much about Dr. Smith as I do now, I would have assumed it was the onset of schizophrenia. I was the right age. His main symptoms were delusions. I identify closely with him in that way.

AP: That's terrifying. I can imagine coming through something like that would make delving into Dr. Smith's story all the more painful. I remember years ago when you first told me about Dr. Smith, you said it was something you wanted to write as well as paint, then at some point you decided to lay out the whole narrative in painting. What was the shift in your thinking?

NS: Pretty sure you said just paint it. Something like that.

AP: Wait, I get credit for this?

NS: And my wife, she said the same. I am a painter after all. That's the deal, right? I went to the Mississippi Museum of Art to do a talk about history and memory and painting after they acquired my *Road to Shubuta* painting about my ancestors and slavery and so on, I think that was 2017. At that point I'd been thinking about Dr. Smith for a couple years without any leads. While I was there, I decided to go to the Department of Archives and History and ask them how I could find out what happened to him. I had a rough date of when he would have been admitted to the Old Asylum, and that was it. They pulled out a giant leather-bound ledger that said "Mississippi Insane Hospital" and I eventually found his entry. I went from there to the museum and told the executive director, Betsy Bradley, that I was going to find out what happened to him and make something about it, and she said I had the museum's support should I need it. Later that same day, I met Stephen Parks, the state librarian. He took it on himself to find anything he could on Dr. Smith in public archives. He had tremendous success over the next couple of years. I cannot overstate how he has unraveled a century-old silence using only records in newspapers, courthouses, chancery clerk office closets. The trail basically ends when Dr. Smith gets into the Old Asylum and his medical records for the next forty years (in the custody of the state of Mississippi) are as yet unfindable. A sequel.

AP: Children are central in the discussion of the work of women painters, and pretty much absent from the discussion of men's work, but your children are so central to your daily life. You paint around them, through them, over them. Can you talk about the impact of fatherhood on your work?

NS: I painted and drew children long before having them, I'm sure from all the children's book illustrations. I think, painting my actual children, so much has changed for me. Maybe images of children used to represent a more imaginative, mystical, or innocent time of life. Children were stand-ins, spectral metaphors. My view of children is a lot more grounded and nuanced now—I see in children responsibility, anxiety, selfless devotion, irritation, trust. They aren't symbols; they are complex concrete wonders who will give you every virus known to man for months on end. They leave no time to dally or flounder. There's constant interruption. Work time is minimal. I've never been so productive.

AP: Speaking of productivity, talk about the Artist Support Pledge project. How long have you been doing it, and what is the relationship to the Dr. Smith project?

NS: A UK artist called Matthew Burrows came up with the idea of the Artist Support Pledge at the beginning of the pandemic to ease the strain on artists who lost their sales. Artists could post works for $200 (or equivalent) on Instagram, and every time you reach $1,000 in sales, you spend $200 on the work of another living artist. That's it, no oversight, no forms. It's a trust-based socialist ideal. When I first saw that, I thought, "I'll cancel everything and just paint every one of Ethel's (that's Dr. Smith's wife, my great-grandmother) photographs—of which I have hundreds—and every story that had surfaced through Stephen's research, and every aspect of optometry, and Mississippi in the 1910s, and mental health in the 1920s, and eugenics. I started making twelve-inch paintings and posting them. Every day they sold within seconds. I don't know how to explain it. I mean, many of them are good, but the world is filled with good things. I needed to generate a ton of imagery and all these people on the internet I don't know very happily sent me money to do so, a gift that I don't think I'll get over. By the time I started painting the giant painting early last year, I had nearly 1,300 images to work from, multiple versions of every scene in his life, having already tested them all in Pledge form. I still make Pledge paintings, yes, I mean, these kids keep eating and food is expensive.

AP: Talk about working in grids.

NS: Sometimes it's a great way to show a lot of small paintings, but in the case of the Dr. Smith project, the grid creates a living organism: pieces come off and are replaced, parts can be sold, parts can be expanded to fit a space.

AP: This speaks to a lack of preciousness and sentimentality which I think of as a hallmark of both your work and your character. It also makes me wonder if Dr. Smith is a project that ends.

NS: Maybe the fluidity of the twenty-first century makes it harder to justify the singular, stable original and it feels better to just let it keep moving and changing. And the grid allows for that. Maybe it's a natural restlessness, or a stubborn unwillingness to just pick a thing. I don't even care for friezes or long cycles. It's frustrating that you can't see it all at once, and it's a logistical hassle to make. But I keep making them. Something about there being a possible before and after to whatever image I'm working on makes me less precious about that image, since it's only a moment in a larger arching reality. If this cycle decides to stay put, I'm happy. If it keeps shedding and regenerating imagery, I'm also happy. Theoretically, I could spend the rest of my life changing out sections of this same painting, replacing vignettes one by one. I'm sure, pretty quickly, Dr. Smith would fade away and another story would emerge. I don't long to paint one thing. I mean, the Pledges, the 1,300 or so paintings? I see them all as one massive painting that is spread in particles around the world, not as individual paintings. I actually dread painting one thing. It's a lot of pressure. ■

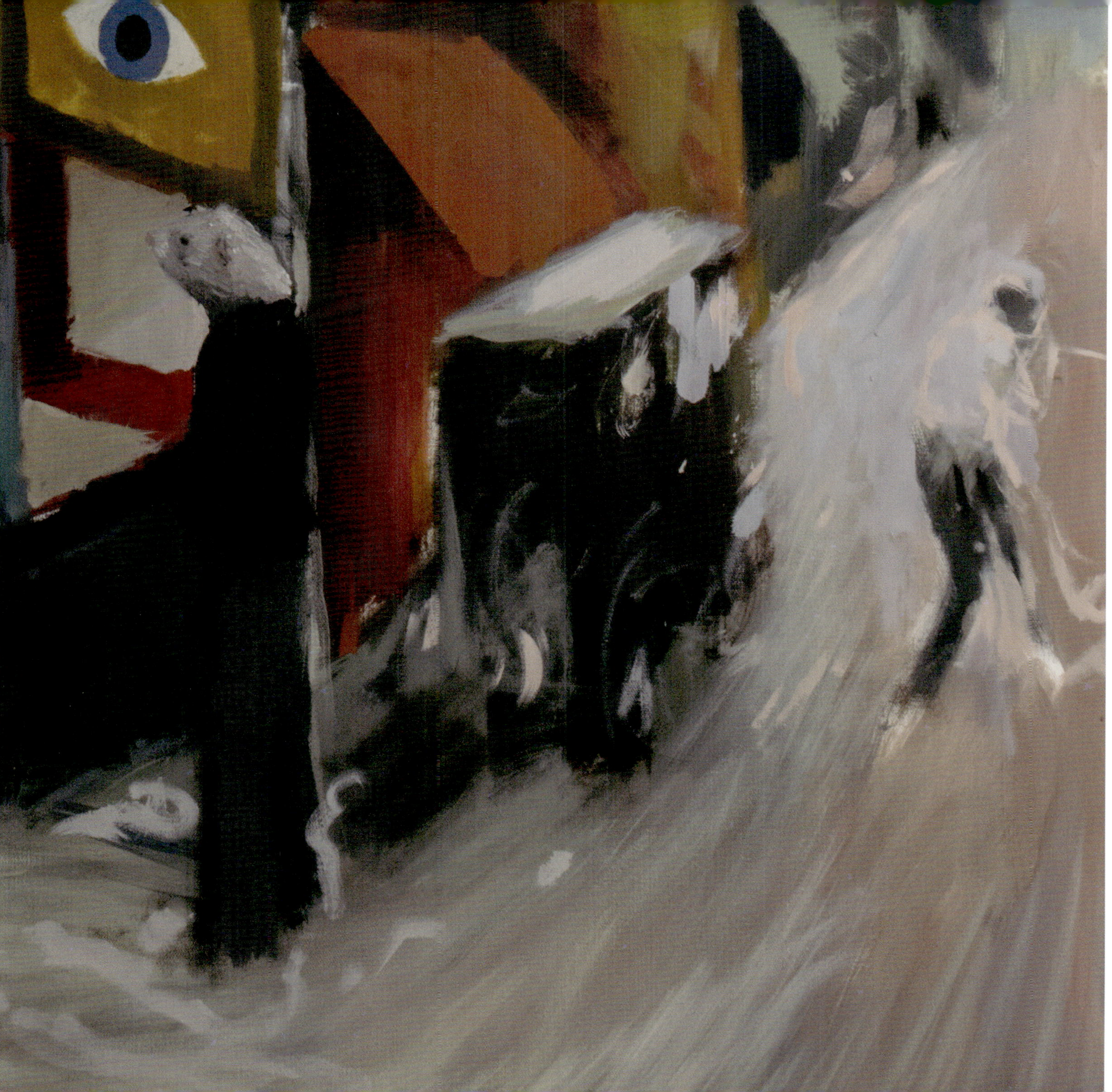

"JUST EVERYTHING": HOW NOAH FILLED HIS ARK

TIMOTHY HYMAN, RA

Man is everywhere a picture-making animal, and the only picture-making animal in the world.
—Frederick Douglass

THE IDEA THAT A PAINTING MIGHT ASPIRE TO BE A BOOK OF LIFE—a single, all-encompassing work that includes all the world—is a kind of eternal recurrence. Even at the end of the twentieth century, when Noah Saterstrom's own art was first taking shape, and when an aesthetic of abstraction or concept appeared so all-dominant, that possibility of painting as a world-creating medium was never entirely abandoned. Some such all-inclusive project remains explicitly present in the astonishing exhibition I encountered here in London only a few days ago, Anselm Kiefer's *Finnegans Wake*, which brings together so many contrasted spaces (the raw archival corridor that might open onto a pile of rubble, or else into a room of gorgeous green-and-gold landscape) as a single vast exploration. When Brian Dillon writes of Joyce's novel as seeming to "contain all words, all thoughts, all histories," and whose "riverine movement begins in the midst of things,"[1] I found myself thinking not only of Kiefer, but of Saterstrom, too.

In undertaking his 122-foot-long world-picture *What Became of Dr. Smith*, Saterstrom is proposing a life journey that transcends its immediate narrative. He is the kind of painter who feels, and is nourished by, the continuity of his medium; so I might find myself bringing to mind the continuous narrative strip of the Bayeux Tapestry or else a pre-Renaissance *predella* (that other more episodic narrative strip of small-scale scenes which fits below the iconic altarpiece). When Frederick Douglass insisted on man's uniqueness as a "picture-making animal,"[2] he was reaching back across the huge range of function that painting continues to fulfil. However sophisticated Saterstrom's knowledge of painting's high history, his abiding love of Bruegel and of Bonnard, he has also internalized the adventures of the untaught artist Henry Darger in *The Realms of the Unreal* (1910–1970) and passionately tracked down the imagery of Southern signboards and local folk art. So, one finds echoes here of many contrasted pictorial languages.

Yet in this essay, the single, panoramic and all-inclusive "ark" I want to take as exemplar for Saterstrom is *The Sala Della Pace (Room of Peace)* frescoed by Ambrogio Lorenzetti in 1337–1340 at the heart of the City-Republic of Siena. Ambrogio's famous wall of *The Well-Governed City and Its Countryside* is, at forty-six feet long, almost five times wider

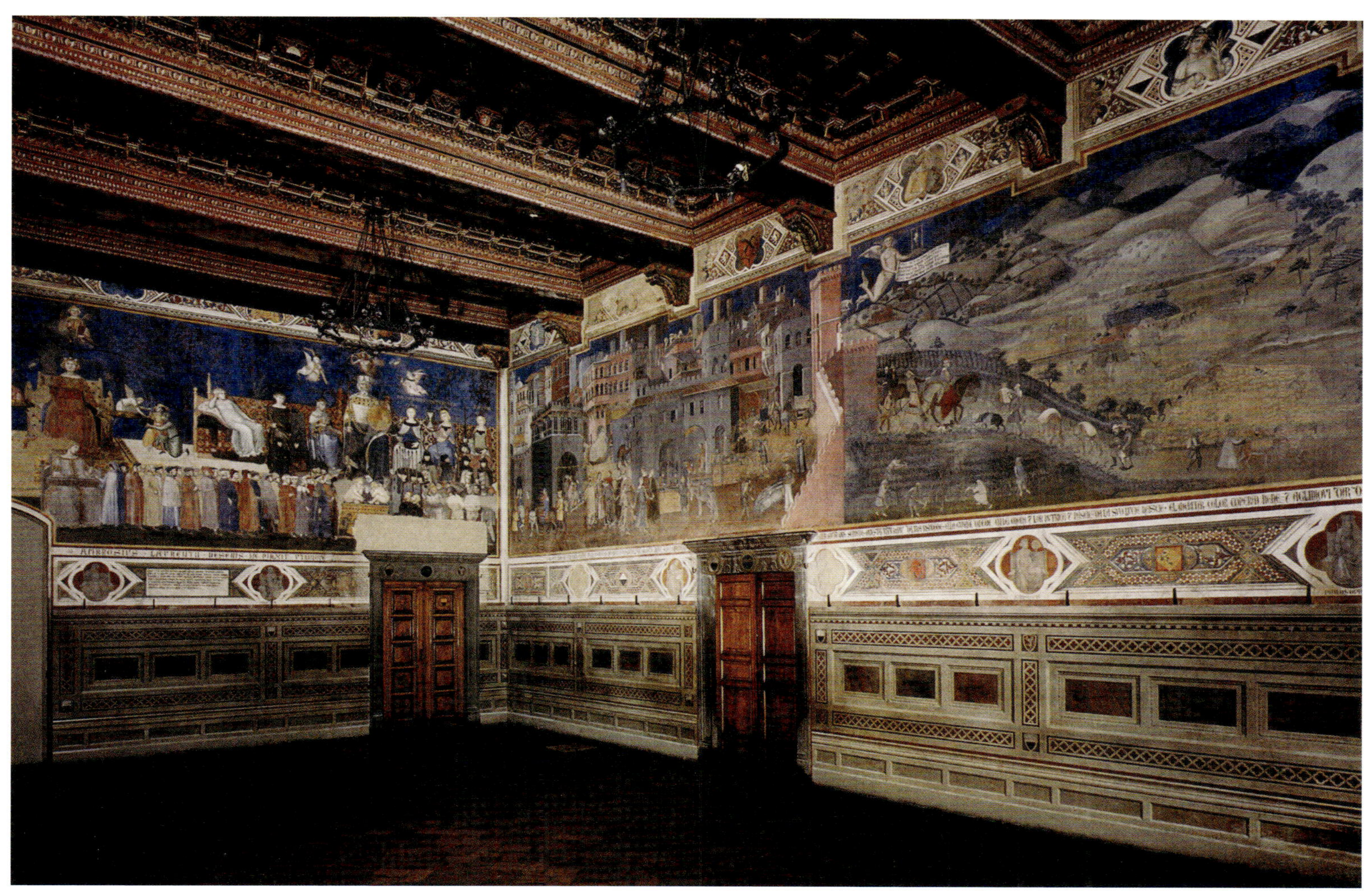

Ambrogio Lorenzetti (Sienese, ca. 1290–1348), Allegory and Effects of Good and Bad Government, *1337–1340. Fresco. Sala della Pace, Palazzo Pubblico, Siena, Italy.*

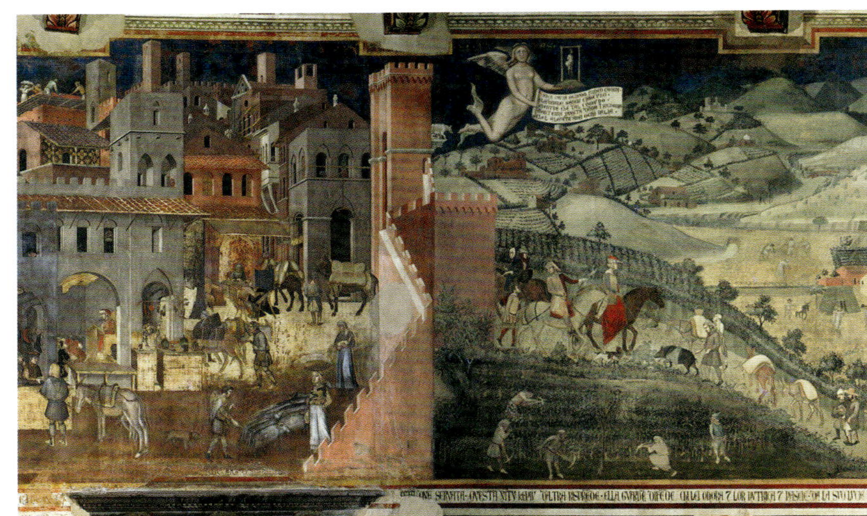

Ambrogio Lorenzetti (Sienese, ca. 1290–1348), Effects of Good Government *(center detail from* Allegory and Effects of Good and Bad Government*), 1337–1340. Fresco. Sala della Pace, Palazzo Pubblico, Siena, Italy / Alinary / Bridgeman Images.*

than it is high. It creates an entire microcosm whose imaginative scope has never been surpassed. We are above the city but we see only the right-hand segment; the city wall must continue far below and to the left, just as the vast tract of countryside (under that curving horizon shared by Saterstrom) must imply an equally grand vista on the other side of the city.

In Ambrogio's pre-perspectival space we are both above *and* inside the city: we see everything, yet we are also able to participate and move freely about. What makes Ambrogio's pictorial space so much more accessible than any of his Renaissance successors is the way near and far can be simultaneously present: at a single glance we might take in the lecturer in the city classroom together with a glimpse of the sea miles beyond. We can recognize a kind of seeing truer to our imaginative experience of space (confirmed in reverie and in dream) than ever possible in single point perspective. And here it may also take on an ethical dimension—embodying the fluidity and social diversity of the libertarian ideal. We are invited to pause at each of the activities our eyes alight on: the bookshop behind the dancers, with a reader in the carrel; the shoe shop, or hosiery; the rapt audience at the lecture; the tavern counter, with its cured hams hanging very much as they do today above Italian bars. Then our eyes may travel upward, catching a woman looking out a side window, a vase of flowers, a birdcage—and high above, the builders at work on the wooden scaffolding, set against the dark sky. Everywhere we notice Ambrogio's relish in chance overlappings: the play of partial donkeys, as headless hindquarters disappear behind houses; the incongruous appearance of a sheep's head jutting forward over a young girl's shoulder. In the vast landscape vista beyond, the effect is of our loosely hovering over the territory, passing from one focus to another, invited to take our journey.

Only one later artist would offer an itinerary quite like this—landscapes of cosmic breadth, crowded cityscapes, executed in a comparable "drawing/painting": whenever I see Ambrogio's figures I think of Pieter Bruegel. One hypothesis is that the young Bruegel, passing through Siena twice, would have encountered Ambrogio's still-famous fresco. Yet the Antwerp Bruegel returned to was now being invaded by a classicizing, idealized landscape convention; and Bruegel has been described as "defending the space of vernacular style"—very much the phrase I might use in identifying Noah Saterstrom's visual idiom across his own enormous narrative strip.

In contrast to Lorenzetti's wonderfully integrated room, Saterstrom's imagery is, like most contemporary art, homeless, without any defined role in society. Even if he speaks of "borrowing heavily" from Giotto or Simone Martini—whose Assisi chapel is perhaps the most perfect of all marriages of painted narrative to architectural setting—he cannot borrow their function. And here the irony enters. Just as his own great-grandfather suffered a lifetime of "mad" displacement, so in our twenty-first century the painter of ambitiously scaled imagery will register some sense of absurdity, of outsiderish and almost comical estrangement.

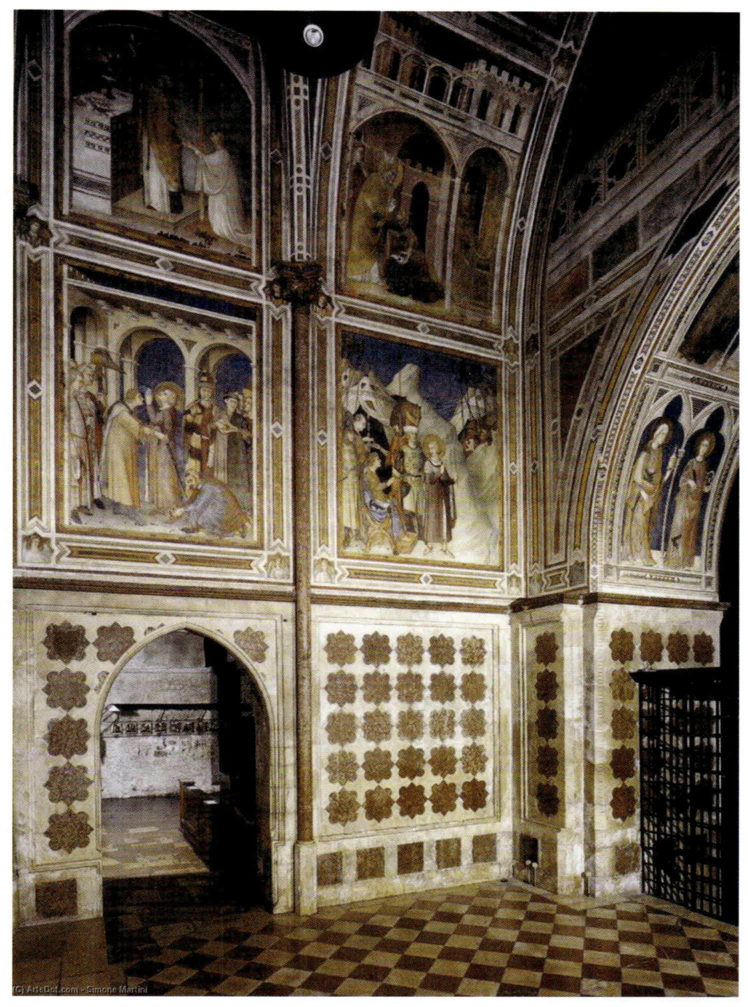

Simone Martini (Sienese, 1284–1344), Scenes from the life of Saint Martin, ca. 1317–1320. Fresco. East wall of the Chapel of Saint Martin, Lower Basilica of San Francesco at Assisi.

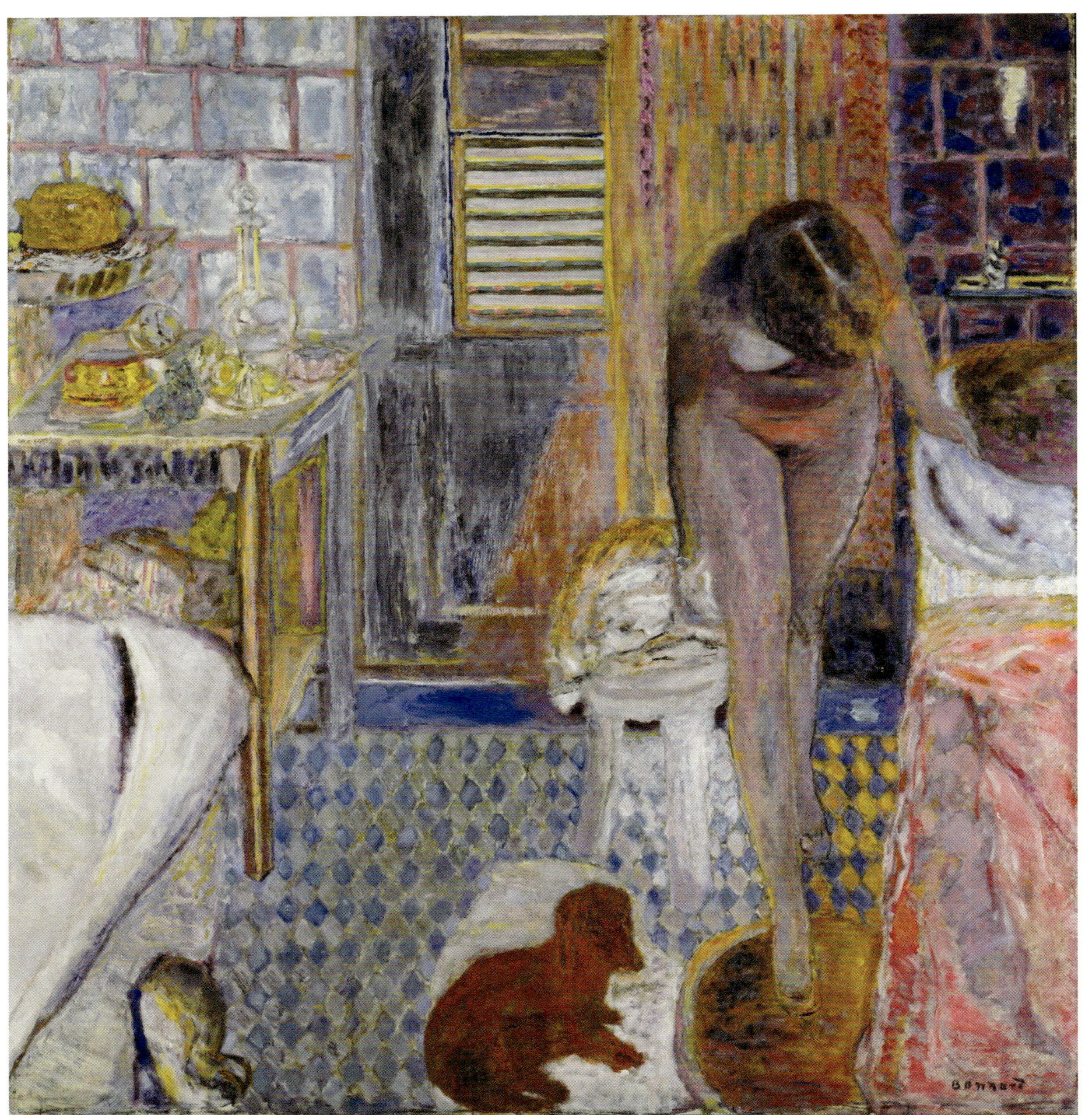
Bonnard

A VERNACULAR FOR THE VOID

What if authentic reality is also discontinuity?
. . . Montage can now work wonders . . . in these
floodplains, these fantastic jungles of the void.
—Ernst Bloch, writing of James Joyce

Saterstrom has spoken of his experience as a postgraduate in Glasgow at the turn of the century; in a class of forty students, seeming the sole painter within a theory-dominated and, in his own words, "viciously anti-sentimental" art culture. I was in Scotland at the same time to preach my itinerant gospel of "Narrative Painting," even if that often appeared a lost cause. I had recently published my first book, a monograph on one of Saterstrom's favorite painters, Pierre Bonnard, emphasizing his radical reinvention of pictorial space.

Pierre Bonnard (French, 1867–1947), La Toilette *(*The Bathroom*), 1932. Oil on canvas, 47 5/8 x 46 1/2 in. The Museum of Modern Art, New York. Florence May Schoenborn Bequest. Digital image © The Museum of Modern Art / Licensed by SCALA / Art Resource, NY. © 2023 Artists Rights Society (ARS), New York.*

What Became of Dr. Smith does sometimes incorporate aspects of Bonnard's tender everyday ("vernacular") language, but sometimes—perhaps more questionably—combined with the realism of the lens.

Although I'm almost thirty years Saterstrom's elder, we've shared the experience of painting's re-emergence after a kind of *tabula rasa*. I think it is evident to most thoughtful painters (even if not perhaps to the general public) that the previous languages of careful representation had become threadbare and unusable. We are all "beginning again" and therefore some tinge of the "primitive" enters into our pictorial idioms. In the same year I met Saterstrom, I'd encountered a refugee from bombed Beirut, whose response to my painting was: "You and your friends, *you all paint like rather damaged children.*"

Back in Nashville, Saterstrom had pursued a strategy of a "Work-a-Day," banged out in several different pictorial idioms; more recently in the era of COVID-19, he has used the Artist Support Pledge to make some 1,300 small paintings, each based on a family snapshot, often in black and white but deftly brought to life, and almost all immediately purchased on Instagram. Yet in parallel he also completed several much larger images in a far more ambitious and "primitive" spatial language—one that incorporates perceptions and

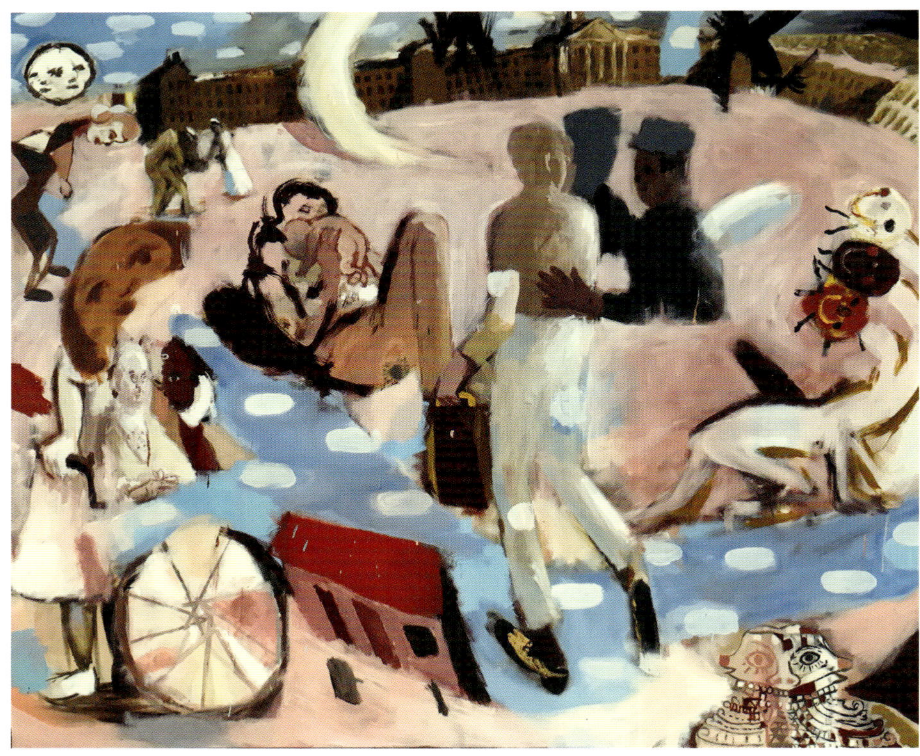

Noah Saterstrom (American, born 1974), Dr. Smith Arrives at the Old Asylum, Jackson, Mississippi, *2018. Oil on canvas, 48 x 60 in. Courtesy of the artist.*

experiences essentially opposed to the photograph. A painting such as *Dr. Smith Arrives at the Old Asylum, Jackson, Mississippi* (2018) (one of several preliminary attempts towards the Dr. Smith theme) allows a place for fractured and fragmentary montage. I might relate it to the quirkier "visionary" space of a painter such as Giovanni di Paolo working in Siena a century after Lorenzetti. In a predella-scene such as *Saint Jerome Appearing to Saint Augustine*, many different spaces are crammed together, with shifts of scale and of psychological states—both the "real" and the hallucinatory. I might have expected, or even hoped, that Saterstrom's enormous project would unfold in a flexible space nearer to that discontinuous idiom. As it has turned out, the chief pictorial language employed is mostly closer to the photographic, perhaps because the lens does supply the main everyday visual vernacular for the general public. Its potential banality is mitigated by the overall structure; *What Became of Dr. Smith* unfolds in a doubling, where road becomes sky becomes river (which I assume to be the Mississippi), the pale blue constantly lost and found, above and below. That double strand leads me to make a specific comparison with

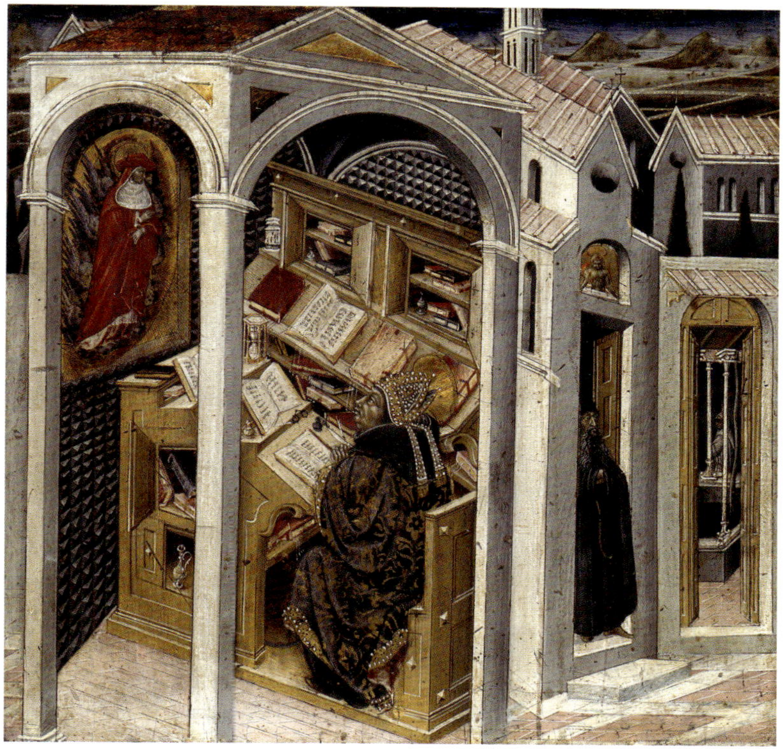

Giovanni di Paolo (Sienese, ca. 1398–1482), Saint Jerome Appearing to Saint Augustine, *ca. 1465. Tempera on wood, 15 3/8 x 19 5/8 in. State Museums of Berlin, Picture Gallery / Jörg P. Anders.*

another contemporary painter, the Mumbai "urban realist" Sudhir Patwardhan. In his large 2007 diptych *Bylanes Saga* (see p. 30), he employs what he has called a "mezzanine," two-tier or "double-decker" structure. As he explains, "I did not want a neutral space . . . I wanted the space itself to respond to the interaction of people."[3]

The obvious danger with lens-based painting is that it becomes "neutral." It will have to compete with many astonishingly inventive video and cinematic narratives. (I am thinking of Lisa Reihana's thirty-two-minute *In Pursuit of Venus [infected]* (2015), where actors play out a tableau of Captain Cook's arrival in New Zealand across a very long screen.) Nevertheless, a world-picture handmade by a single artist does remain a wonderful option. The conventional camera mode (the Kodak forty-degree space that replicates classical perspective, and which Kirk Varnedoe once dubbed a "little Brunelleschi box") is evidently acceptable to our selfie-obsessed contemporaries, even if its suppression of all peripheral vision seems utterly unlike my experience of seeing. Bonnard called his art "the transcription of the adventures of the optic nerve"; yet a more "regular" pictorial space is so ingrained

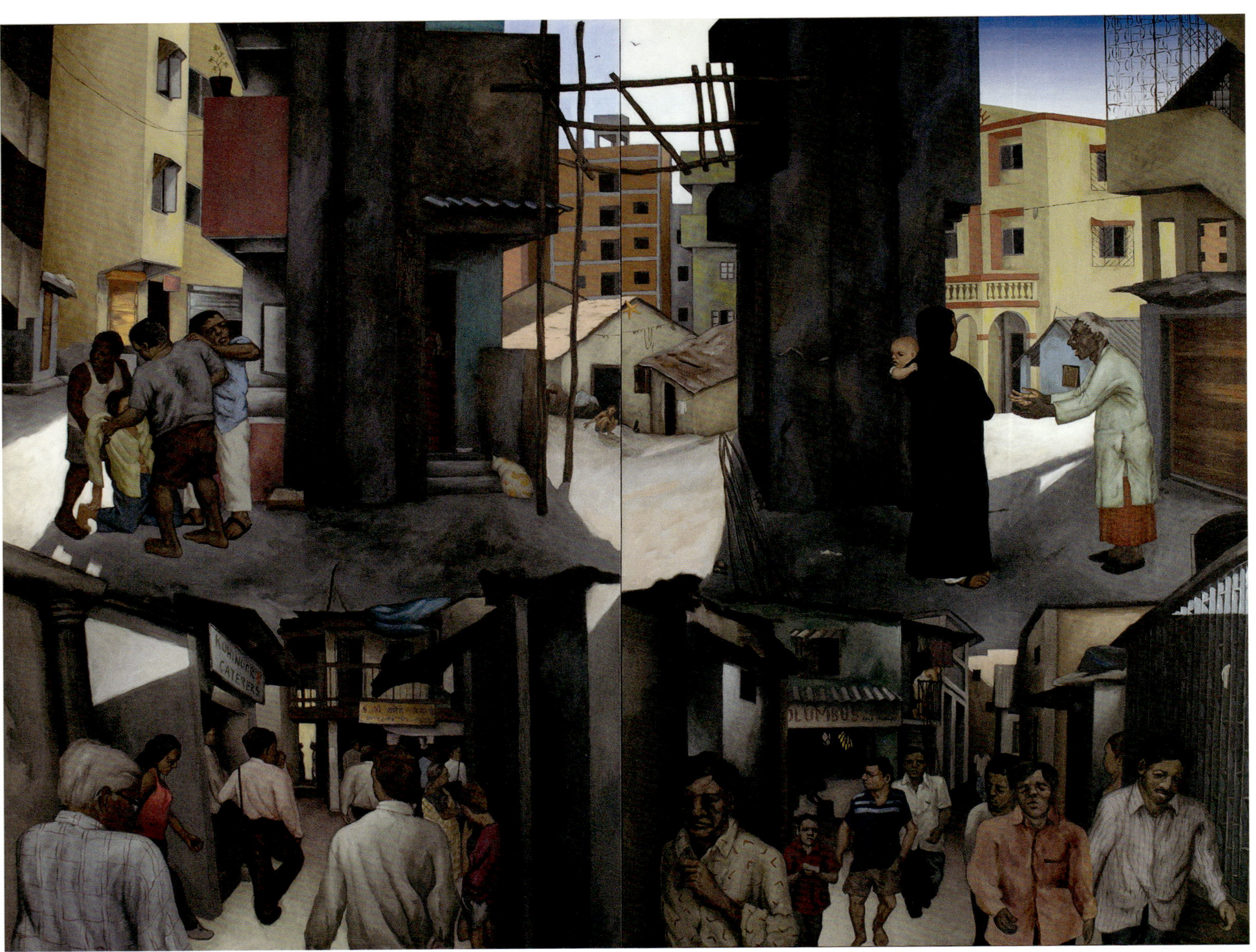
KOHINOOR CATERERS
OLUMBUS

Sudhir Patwardhan (Indian, born 1949), Bylanes Saga, *2007. Acrylic on canvas, 72 x 96 in. Private Collection. Courtesy of the artist and Vadehra Art Gallery.*

that viewers often see his work as distorted.[4] (The painter Paula Rego admonished both Bonnard and me for perpetrating "wonky" images.)

Dr. Smith was after all an optometrist, for whom the lens was all important, whatever its limitations. His profession was to restore "normal" sight. His great-grandson is somewhat of a visionary and has spoken of episodes of mental illness that include hallucination. When I first saw photographs of the entire work, I questioned whether the final section—a green and white near-idyll with a cutaway view of the "good" mental asylum where Dr. Smith spent his final thirty years—might appear a little bland as a conclusion. To my amazement, Saterstrom sent almost by return his new addition of a giant figure, the hundred-eyed god Argos. I think the whole tenor of this image, which is essentially a narrative of Recovery, was thereby altered: Documentation yields to Imagination.

A great modern novel consists of and ought to consist of just everything.
—John Cowper Powys, writing of Dostoevsky

One chief model for the maker of a modern pictorial "ark" is to be found not in visual art but in literature. One could nominate a huge range of all-encompassing works, from the Bible to Dante, from *Don Quixote* to *War and Peace*, and from the past century or so, among those I've found most rewarding: Robert Musil's *The Man Without Qualities*, Ezra Pound's *The Cantos*, James Joyce's *Ulysses*, John Cowper Powys' *A Glastonbury Romance*, Marcel Proust's *In Search of Lost Time*, William Faulkner's *Absalom, Absalom!* Each has enough of the cosmological to be described as "visionary"—or as an "Epic-of-Fragmentation." Visual language can morph "reality" with delusion or dream just as effectively as any novel. Saterstrom's cradle-to-grave narrative of Dr. Smith is a recovery not only of a lost family history but also of the possibilities within painting. ■

[1] Brian Dillan, "Anselm Kiefer – Finnegans Wake," White Cube, 2023, www.whitecube.com/gallery-exhibitions/anselm-kiefer-finnegans-wake.

[2] Frederick Douglass, "Lecture on Pictures," in *Picturing Frederick Douglass: An Illustrated Biography of the Nineteenth Century's Most Photographed American*, eds. John Stauffer, Zoe Trodd, and Celeste-Marie Bernier (New York: W.W. Norton & Company, 2015), 131.

[3] Sudhir Patwardhan in discussion with Nancy Adajania and Timothy Hyman, January 11, 2020, National Gallery of Modern Art, Mumbai.

[4] "La Peinture ou la transcription des aventures du nerf optique." Diary note for 1 Feb. 1934, quoted in *Bonnard*, exh. cat. (Paris: Centre Georges Pompidou, 1984), p. 190, trans. in *Bonnard*, exh. cat. (Washington: The Phillips Collection, 1984), p. 69.

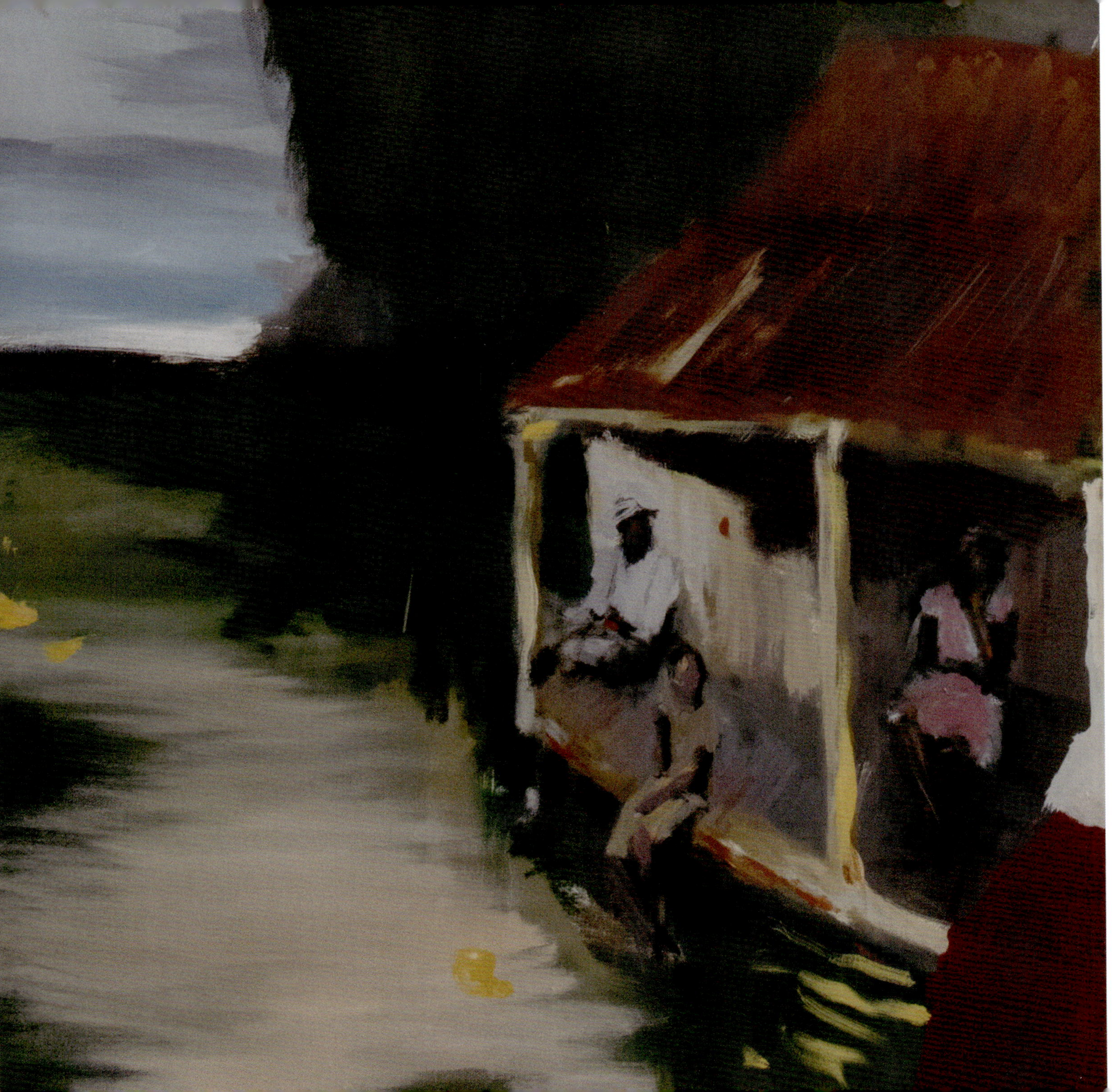

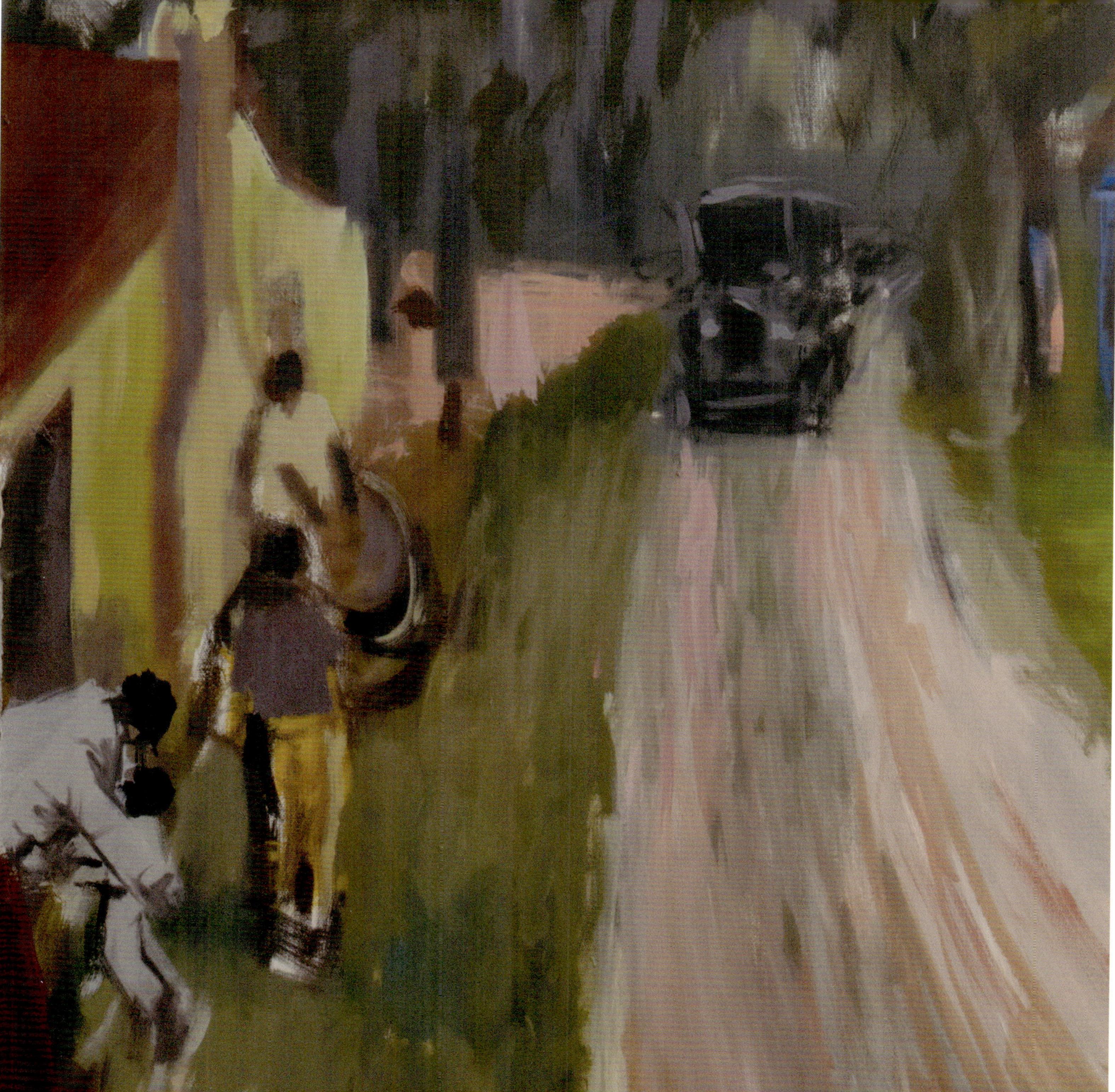

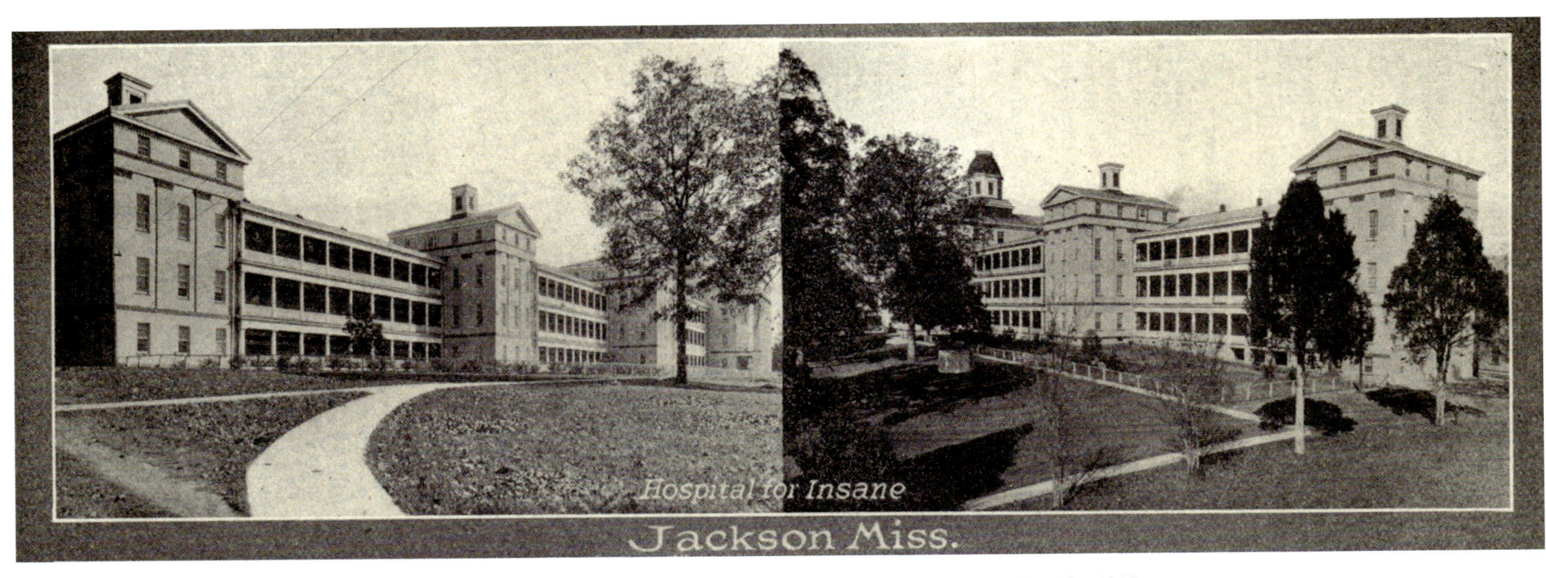

Mississippi State Insane Hospital, as pictured in Illinois Central *magazine, December 1915.*

THE MISSISSIPPI STATE HOSPITAL:
FROM BOOM TO BUST, 1855–1935

AMY FORBES, PHD, AND PATRICK HOPKINS, PHD

THE MISSISSIPPI STATE LUNATIC ASYLUM[1] was conceived in the 1840s to provide humane treatment to people with mental illness and address what today would be considered other types of medical or social issues like epilepsy, puerperal fever, or addiction. Its origins lie in the Enlightenment-era transition from family care or prison to large public asylums and similar institutions as the customary approach to treating society's mentally ill and supposedly incurable individuals. In 1846, Governor Albert G. Brown (whose relatives later attempted to forcibly admit him to the asylum) requested a state appropriation of $10,000 and land for the construction of the institution. When famed reformer Dorothea Dix traveled to Mississippi to survey the conditions of the state's mentally disabled population as part of this effort, she described them living in squalor in "wretched poverty-stricken dwellings" and "dungeons of county jails," an observation that helped secure sufficient funding to build the asylum.[2]

The asylum was built in 1855 as a leading-edge institution. From its inception, it occupied important space in Mississippi, both geographically and culturally. Built on a hill just north of Jackson, it was an impressive edifice for the capital city. Many hoped that, as a monument to humanitarian care and progressive thinking, the institution might prove the honor of the slaveholding state to abolitionist critics,[3] and perhaps to Mississippians themselves. Subsequently, however, patient overcrowding, underfunding, and the failure of psychiatry to achieve meaningful cures tarnished the hospital's gleaming image.[4]

MENTAL ILLNESS TREATMENT BEFORE THE ASYLUM

From the colonial period through the early nineteenth century, the landscape of mental health care in Mississippi, as in America generally, was characterized by a profound absence of adequate support and understanding for individuals grappling with mental illnesses. Prior to the establishment of specialized mental health institutions, individuals with mental illnesses or cognitive impairments relied primarily on care provided by their families. This was especially true in rural areas like Mississippi. The prevailing attitudes of the time held that most individuals with mental illnesses were beyond cure, which significantly contributed to the deplorable conditions in which they were kept. At the heart of the issue was the fundamental belief that mental illness was induced primarily by moral or spiritual failings. Consequently, people with mental illness and their families often faced punishment and shame as opposed to medical treatment and compassion. Some families chose to hide their relatives with mental illness in attics or sheds to avoid social embarrassment, escape possible stigma associated with mental illness, or simply control fractious or harmful behavior.

Family care was neither comprehensive nor guaranteed. For those with no family, or whose families were unable or unwilling to provide care at home, destitution often loomed, forcing sufferers of mental illness into a state of dependency, where they resorted to vagabondage and begging for sustenance and shelter. Some individuals found themselves in the grim confines of workhouses or prisons, exacerbating their adversities. These institutions lacked humane treatment and focused instead on confinement in chains, straitjackets, and forced drugging.

Their care, or the lack thereof, mirrored broader medical practices of the time, which were based on rudimentary treatments such as bloodletting and purgatives. Thus, through the early nineteenth century, the state of mental health care in Mississippi was characterized by a lack of understanding, compassion, and treatment opportunities for individuals suffering from mental illnesses.

RISE OF THE THERAPEUTIC ASYLUM IN THE EARLY NINETEENTH CENTURY

In the early nineteenth century, multiple social factors led to alternatives to the prevailing punitive and neglectful approaches to mental health care. As the United States rapidly transitioned from an agrarian society to an industrialized one, the pressures of urbanization and increased population density brought mental illness to the forefront as a pressing social issue.

The first modern American mental asylums were built in the industrializing Northeast, including Pennsylvania, New Jersey, and New York. But even in more rural, Southern states, growing cities raised concerns about the potential threat to public safety posed by individuals with mental illnesses, prompting a reevaluation of how society addressed these challenges. Additionally, new intellectual and moral movements brought changing attitudes toward individuals with mental illness. Enlightenment ideals that emphasized reason, empathy, and human rights initiated a departure from punitive and degrading treatment. As society increasingly recognized the intrinsic value and humanity of individuals with mental illnesses, there was a growing consensus that more compassionate and effective care was not only a moral imperative but also essential for the well-being of society as a whole.

The most significant facilitator of change was the emergence of "moral treatment" as a humane alternative to the established practices of the time. Moral treatment emphasized the importance of providing compassionate care and emotional guidance to individuals with mental illnesses, challenging the widespread notion that these individuals were morally or spiritually deficient. This approach acknowledged the inherent dignity of people with mental illness and aimed to facilitate their recovery through therapeutic and emotional interventions. The therapy contested the prevailing demonological theories regarding mental illness and underscored the significance of one's surroundings in shaping one's character, positing that unfavorable external conditions had the potential to induce mental instability. The moral treatment framework held an optimistic view that a suitable environment could be instrumental in facilitating recovery. A fundamental tenet of this doctrine was the acknowledgment of a physiological foundation for mental disorders, asserting that insanity was primarily the result of brain damage.

By the early nineteenth century, a profound transformation in the approach to mental health care was underway, seen in the pioneering efforts of eighteenth-century physicians such as Philippe Pinel, William Tuke, and Benjamin Rush. These visionary medical practitioners established benevolent institutions and hospitals dedicated to the scientific treatment of the insane. In France, Pinel's revolutionary work at La Bicêtre advocated for the removal of chains and the implementation of humane treatment practices. In England, Tuke, a member of the Quaker community, founded the Retreat in York, a private mental hospital that created an approach to treatment of people with mental illness within the framework of the Quaker Society of Friends. The treatment provided at the York Retreat advocated personalized care and compassion with a central focus on restoring residents' self-esteem and self-control. Notably, the institution was an early proponent of occupational therapy, offering residents activities such as leisurely walks and farm labor in serene and tranquil environments.

These new ideas gained traction in the American colonies through Benjamin Rush, a Philadelphia Quaker and European-educated physician frequently referred to as "the Father of American Psychiatry" for writing the first systematic textbook on mental diseases in America.[5]

A leading advocate of medical and political advancement, Rush was a signer of the Declaration of Independence, surgeon in the Continental Army during the American Revolution, treasurer of the US Mint, as well as a private physician. He believed that mental illness resulted from physical problems with blood vessels in the brain. His treatment methods combined old methods of bleeding and purging with warm baths and tranquil environments. Rush's advocacy for the moral and medical treatment of the mentally ill, as well as his establishment of the Pennsylvania Hospital in 1751, laid the groundwork for a more compassionate and scientifically informed approach to mental health care in the US. His pioneering efforts represented a turning point in the history of mental health care, paving the way for the development of institutions dedicated to the humane and scientifically sound treatment of mental illness.

THE MISSISSIPPI STATE LUNATIC ASYLUM

When the Mississippi State Lunatic Asylum opened its doors in 1855, it was a landmark establishment in the realm of mental health care as the first state institution in Mississippi designed for the care of individuals with mental illness. The asylum was the creation of Drs. William S. Langley, Edward Pickett, and Thomas J. Catchings, leading lights of the state's medical community. The physicians conceived of the institution as a means of caring for its most vulnerable citizens and, with its formation, they hoped to demonstrate Mississippi's place in civil society. Construction took nearly a decade, hindered by appropriation disputes within the state legislature, fires, and an epidemic.

The blueprint for the Mississippi State Insane Asylum was crafted by local architect Joseph Willis, who drew inspiration from the New Jersey State Lunatic Asylum. This facility, erected in 1848, adhered to the "Kirkbride plan," a comprehensive and holistic approach to the treatment of mental illness conceptualized by Dr. Thomas Story Kirkbride. Dr. Kirkbride, a Quaker physician, architect, and advocate for the curability and humane treatment of the mentally ill, created a plan for treating mental illness that linked therapy for patients in an asylum to the architecture of the buildings. His plan became the touchstone of mental health care for much of the century, with forty such institutions built by 1880. The Mississippi asylum was just the sixth Kirkbride institution in the nation, and the first in the South.

Kirkbride's treatise *On the Construction, Organization, and General Arrangements of Hospitals for the Insane with Some Remarks on Insanity and Its Treatment*, published in 1854, offered meticulous directives for the design of mental institutions, encompassing elements ranging from the architectural layout, building materials, landscaping of the surroundings, and ventilation and drainage systems, to patient activities, doctor-patient contact, musical activities, and hospital decor.[6] Asylums were designed as expansive, well-lit structures, situated on estates spanning at least 100 acres, which provided patients with both aesthetically pleasing grounds and opportunities for agricultural activities. Central to Kirkbride's philosophy was the promotion of moral treatment in a therapeutic environment characterized by pleasant surroundings, outdoor labor, social interactions, personal hygiene, and intellectual stimulation, all of which could aid in the recovery of individuals with mental illness more effectively than punitive confinement and outdated medical treatments such as bloodletting and purging.

Kirkbride underscored the importance of creating an asylum that exuded a cheerful and comfortable atmosphere, eschewing prison-like features and concealing security measures. He called for maintaining patient populations within manageable limits, stressing that overcrowding could adversely affect patient welfare. He suggested that no more than 250 patients should be confined in a single institution. Each asylum should be subdivided into distinct wards, with an average of fifteen patients in each, and outfitted with various amenities to ensure the well-being of residents.

Like all Kirkbride asylums, the Mississippi asylum had a central administration building flanked by two wings—one for men, one for women—in a batwing shape. Tiered wards separated residents by the type of condition. More excitable patients were placed on lower floors and farthest from the central administrative structure, with quieter, less fractious patients situated in the upper floors and closer to the administrative center. Ideally, this linear arrangement would make the patients' asylum experience more comfortable and productive by isolating them from other patients with illnesses antagonistic to their own. The linear architecture allowed fresh air, natural light, and views of the asylum grounds from all sides of each ward, all the way to the end of the wings.

The Mississippi asylum housed about 150 patients in its early years, well within Kirkbride's stipulated ceiling. Gardens served to stimulate patients' minds with natural beauty (enhanced by rational order) while improving the overall appearance of the asylum. Farmland made the

Report of the Officers of the Lunatic Asylum, Wm. B. Williamson, Superintendent, November 2, 1857.

PREDISPOSING CAUSES OF MENTAL ALBERATION SO FAR AS COULD BE ASCERTAINED.

Hereditary Tendency	13
Epelepsy	13
Domestic Troubles	8
Ill Health	6
Dissipation	3
Uterine Irritation	3
Pecuniary Troubles	2
Change of Life	2
Love	1
Exposure	1
Military Ambition	1
Paralysis	1
Yellow Feaver	1
Religious excitement	1
Blow on the head	1
Not known	39

asylum more self-sufficient by providing readily available food and other products at a minimal cost to the state. Patients who were able worked the farm and helped keep the grounds. Kirkbride believed this kind of structured activity would provide a sense of purpose and responsibility that would help regulate the mind and improve physical fitness. Patients were also encouraged to take part in recreational activities, games, and entertainment which would further engage their minds and help with social skills. One of the superintendents, Dr. Compton, believed that dancing was a particularly healthy activity. Dance lessons and great balls were held at the asylum, not just for patients but also for members of the Jackson public.

The hospital housed a broad spectrum of patients. Superintendents' reports, issued annually then biennially, listed conditions that led to admission to the asylum, including many that today would not necessarily warrant hospitalization. The 1857 report, for instance, cited hereditary causes, domestic troubles, love, military ambition, religious excitement, epilepsy, and situational depression. The hospital cared for people on the fringes of society before there were other kinds of social safety nets available, as well as for people with infections or injuries. For example, women with puerperal fever, an infection after childbirth, regularly entered the asylum, as did patients with head injuries and pellagra, a disease caused by niacin deficiency that leads to dementia in advance stages.

It is important to emphasize that a significant portion of individuals admitted to the asylum were released following treatment. These positive outcomes were attributed to the administration of effective medical care, improved nutritional provisions, and the acquisition of skills for self-management of their conditions. Many of them underwent medical treatment and left after experiencing notable improvements in their health. Superintendents' records indicate that of the approximately 30,000 patients at the hospital between 1855 and 1935, about one third died there. Patients who passed away without being claimed by their families were laid to rest on the asylum grounds in a cemetery (now being studied[7]) organized in orderly rows, each marked by a wooden grave indicator.

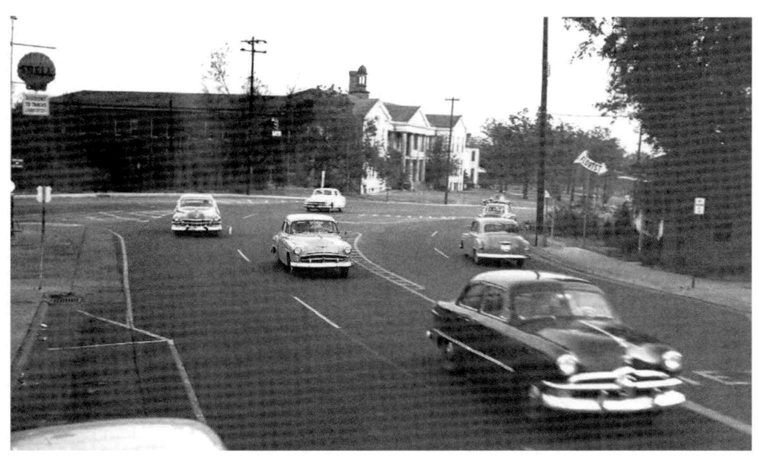

Pictured here in ca. 1950, the Cottage Building was built ca. 1915 to address the growing number of patients. Following the hospital's relocation to Whitfield, this building was used for state offices before its demolition in 1956. Photo: Lefleur's Bluff Heritage Foundation, courtesy of Mrs. Helene Rotwein.

EXPANSION AND OVERCROWDING

Around the turn of the twentieth century, overcrowding became a problem at the asylum due to its successes and demand for its services, its practices of inclusion, and a lack of sufficient funding. Additionally, the facility's large, open architecture belied its capacity, appearing as if it could always accommodate more patients. By 1870, during the Reconstruction era, the institution began admitting Black patients on a regular basis. Until that time, the hospital had been open almost exclusively to white patients, with some enslaved and free Black patients admitted by special request of the board of trustees. At the onset of World War I, the population of patients by race was approximately sixty percent Black and forty percent white. In early 1918 the hospital housed a patient population of 1,624, including 909 Black patients and 715 white patients.[8] The asylum remained racially segregated throughout its history.

As the asylum's patient population increased, so too did its facilities and capacity for self-sustenance. By the year 1935, with 2,600 residents, the 1,300-acre campus included not only the core asylum buildings but also diverse agricultural operations. The institution boasted fruit orchards, productive gardens, substantial livestock operations, poultry farming, and an expansive dairy. The administration, particularly the superintendents and senior staff members, regularly documented and emphasized these endeavors, reflecting the institution's commitment to self-sufficiency. Agricultural operations played a pivotal role in the recovery of patients, many of whom arrived in a malnourished state. The hospital also offered surgical and dental care, and the campus included a medical laboratory.

As early as the 1870s, it was clear that the institution was becoming overcrowded. As part of the state's solution to ease overpopulation, the East Mississippi State Hospital opened in Meridian in 1882, but it, too, reached capacity soon after opening. The Kirkbride plan collapsed under the weight of such overcrowding, curtailing its interrelated housing arrangements, therapeutic program, and clinical outcomes. It was replaced by the cottage model, in which groups of cottages accommodated patients and attempted to promote therapeutic social interaction. New buildings housed more patients but overcrowding continued. Securing funding became increasingly challenging due to waning confidence among legislators and the public regarding the treatment of incurable cases over the long term. Despite declining conditions, superintendents kept the need for mental health care on the front burner of state politics, eventually convincing legislators that a new facility was required for adequate care. In 1935, the Old Asylum closed and its 2,464 patients transferred to the new Mississippi State Hospital at Whitfield, fifteen miles outside of Jackson.[9] ■

Eudora Welty (1909–2001), Abandoned "Lunatic Asylum," Jackson, *1936 negative, 1980 print. 10 3/4 x 11 1/8 in. Collection of Mississippi Museum of Art, Jackson. Gift of Mr. and Mrs. Richard L. Miller. 2000.023. Photo: Mark Geil. © Eudora Welty, LLC; Courtesy Eudora Welty Collection–Mississippi Department of Archives and History.*

[1] The hospital opened in 1855 as the Mississippi State Lunatic Asylum. In 1900 legislators renamed it the Mississippi State Insane Hospital, though references to "the asylum" continued well into the twentieth century. Today scholars commonly refer to the hospital as the Mississippi State Asylum or the "Old Asylum" to distinguish it from the new hospital that opened outside of Jackson in 1935. In this essay, the terms "hospital" and "asylum" are used interchangeably.

[2] Dorothea L. Dix, "Memorial Soliciting Adequate Appropriations for the Construction of a State Hospital for the insane in the State of Mississippi, February, 1850," in *On Behalf of the Insane Poor: Selected Reports*, ed. David J. Rothman (New York: Arno Press and *The New York Times*, 1971), 5.

[3] Eugene Allan Branstiter, *Madness, Scalawagery, and Reconstruction: Dr. William M. Compton and Civil War Era Politics* (Master's thesis, University of Southern Mississippi, 2013).

[4] Whitney E. Barringer, *The Corruption of Promise: The Insane Asylum in Mississippi, 1848–1910* (PhD dissertation, University of Mississippi, 2016).

[5] Benjamin Rush, *Medical Inquiries and Observations upon Disease of the Mind* (Philadelphia: Grigg, 1830).

[6] See also Nancy Tomes, *The Art of Asylum-Keeping: Thomas Story Kirkbride and the Origins of American Psychiatry* (Philadelphia: University of Pennsylvania Press, 1994) and Katherine Ziff, *Asylum on the Hill: History of a Healing Landscape* (Athens, Ohio: Ohio University Press, 2012).

[7] See asylumhillproject.org.

[8] *Biennial Report of the Mississippi State Insane Hospital, 1917 to 1919*, 11. The hospital remained racially segregated at both its original and post-1935 locations until the Civil Rights Act of 1964.

[9] *Biennial Report of the Mississippi State Insane Hospital, 1933–1935*, 6.

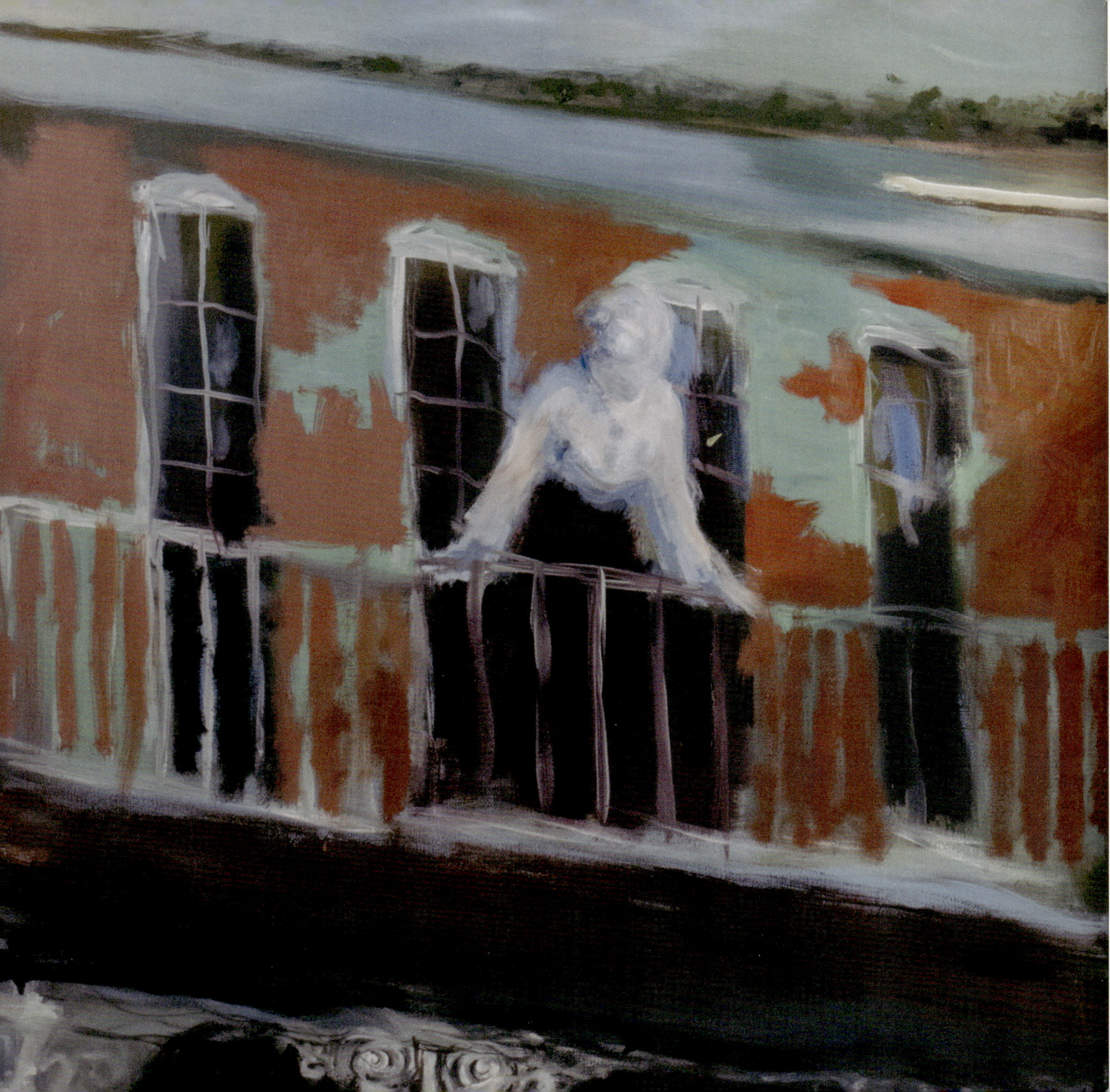

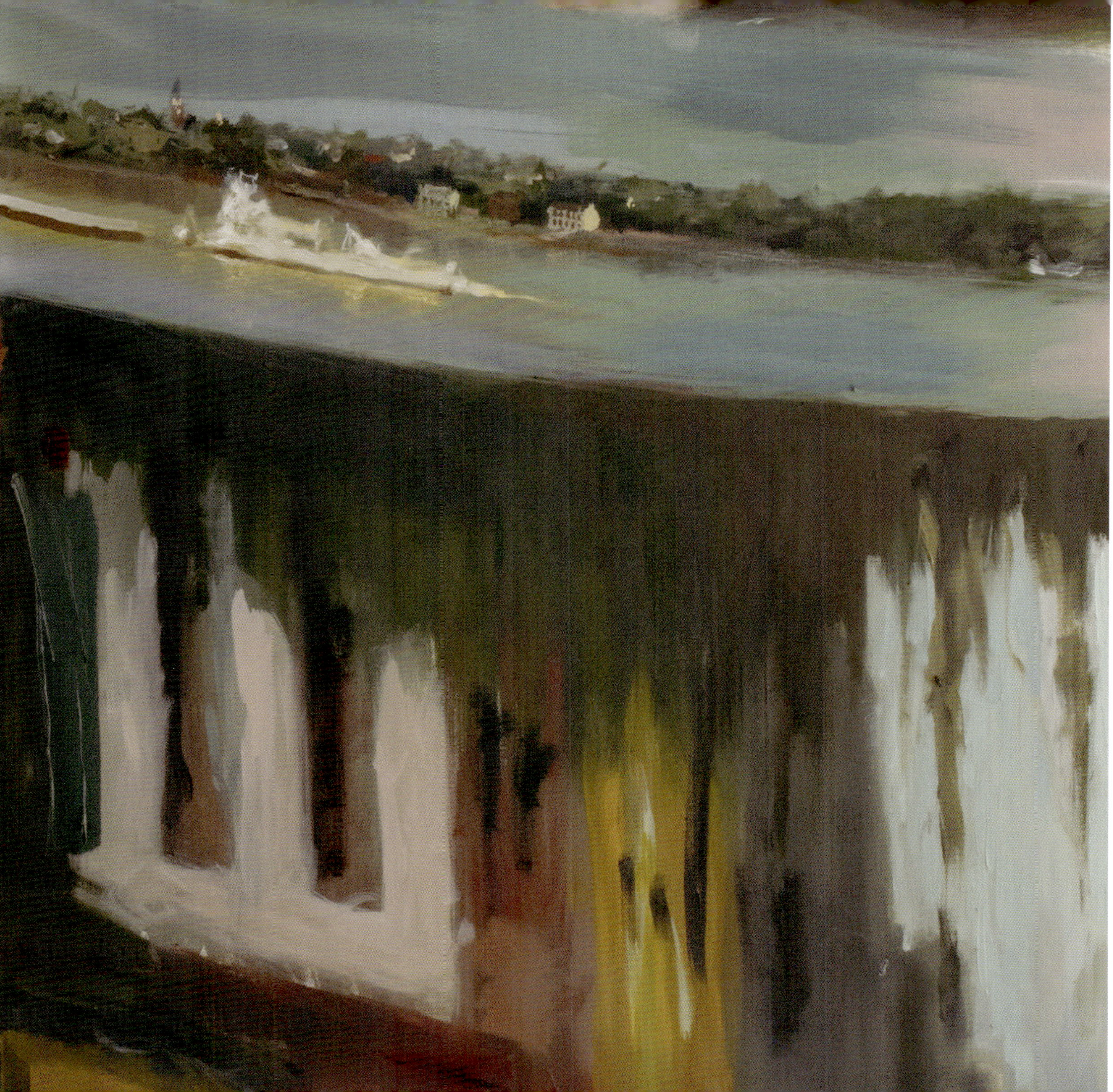

THE STORY OF DR. SMITH

AS TOLD BY NOAH SATERSTROM

based on information culled from family histories and public archives

circa 1890 J.T. Smith, a druggist prone to "mental aberrations" and violent rages, marries Minnie Lemmon and opens an apothecary shop in Louisiana.

1891 David Lawson Lemmon Smith is born to Minnie and J.T. Smith in Donaldsonville, Louisiana.

1894 Ethel Brandon is born in Natchez, Mississippi, to Daisy Patterson and Gerard Brandon IV, prominent lawyer and grandson of Mississippi's fourth governor.

1898 J.T. Smith is committed to the Louisiana State Asylum. Two months later, Minnie receives word of his death. In fact, J.T. Smith has escaped incarceration and faked his death, having a coffin sent to Minnie as proof of his demise. J.T. was alleged to have died of yellow fever and thus his coffin was sealed, preventing Minnie from viewing her husband's remains.

1901 J.T. Smith resurfaces when Minnie attempts to remarry, writing to his brother-in-law, "She thinks me dead," and demanding he stop the union. There are no records of his future movements.

1904 The drugstore Minnie has run since J.T.'s disappearance burns to the ground in a massive fire. The event is deemed suspicious but never confirmed as arson.

1913 David attends optometry school in New Orleans.

1914 David, now styling himself "Dr. Smith," works as an itinerant optometrist throughout southern Louisiana and Mississippi.

1915 Dr. Smith meets Ethel Brandon when work brings him to Natchez. The couple attends a ball at the Prentiss Club, falling in love during a whirlwind romance.

Dr. Smith opens an optical shop on Main Street in Natchez.

The first inklings of illness are seen in Smith's writings and letters, as he shares vague, disquieting feelings of persecution.

1916 Dr. Smith and Ethel marry in Natchez. They are featured regularly in the *Natchez Democrat*'s society pages.

Dr. Smith and Ethel move to Vicksburg, where he opens the Dr. Smith Optical Company on Washington Street.

Away from her family for the first time and newly pregnant, Ethel writes hundreds of letters to her mother and family.

1917 Margaret Gerard Smith is born to Ethel and Dr. Smith, who does not attend the birth. Later, he writes to Ethel of his regret at missing his daughter's birth. In the same letter, he describes being tormented by a blind man who sings incessantly outside his shop.

circa 1916–1919 Numerous meetings to establish "the best way to breed" are held in Vicksburg, echoing a national conversation around eugenics. Southern women's clubs take up this mantle and focus on rooting out people they deem to be degenerates—criminals, addicts, homosexuals, and the "feeble minded."

1920 Dr. Smith becomes head of the Mississippi Association of Optometrists. He writes articles about optometry that Ethel edits.

circa 1920s Dr. Smith's articles voice a particular dislike for itinerant spec-peddlers, whom he compares to snake oil salesmen. His essays published in optometry journals relay his stance that high-quality optometry should be available to all. Several peers take exception to Dr. Smith's sharp criticisms and views about universal access; henceforth, he characterizes these people as his "enemies."

circa 1920 Dr. Smith's letters mention his belief that he is being forced to work as a "breeder" for the US Secret Service. His concerns center on birth defects.

circa 1919–1921 Dr. Smith invents and builds his optical truck. Outfitted with a waiting room, exam room, and grinding room, it is a one-stop shop for all optometric needs. He envisions traveling to rural Mississippi and Louisiana, providing free exams, and only charging for purchased spectacles. Dr. Smith makes it a point to advertise that he treats everyone, providing equal care to all regardless of race or class.

1921 Dr. Smith's traveling shop opens, but he is immediately shut down and repeatedly fined. Legislation has been passed not only to prevent spec-peddlers from defrauding customers but also to prevent itinerant optometrists from practicing in Mississippi. Dr. Smith believes this legislation to be advanced by the "enemies" who disagree with his inclusive treatment practices.

The loss of his livelihood appears to accelerate Dr. Smith's psychosis. He becomes convinced that prominent lawyers and businessmen in Mississippi are embezzling his money and that the Secret Service is doping him remotely.

His savings depleted and past support from Ethel's father gone, Dr. Smith sends Ethel, seven-year-old Margaret, and their three younger children, Mary Jane, Helen, and David Jr., to Shreveport. He tells Ethel the move is for the family's safety but does not accompany them. The children never see their father again. Dr. Smith continues to practice in his truck throughout Louisiana.

1924 In September, Dr. Smith checks in to a hotel in Port Gibson, Mississippi, where he sets up a temporary shop for conducting exams. A fifteen-year-old girl, after visiting the mobile office, accuses Smith of raping her. He is immediately set upon by a mob of angry farmers that includes the victim's father, uncles, and cousins. The mob beats Dr. Smith, transports him to nearby Hermanville, and attempts to lynch him. Just before he is to be hanged, the Claiborne County sheriff intervenes and Dr. Smith is arrested.

1924–1925 Unable to furnish bond, Dr. Smith is jailed from September to January. He writes numerous letters during this period, with one addressed to the governor of Mississippi. In it, he requests protection and asserts he is being persecuted by his enemies for a crime he didn't commit.

1925 Dr. Smith writes to his father, who he heretofore claimed was dead. The language is coherent but the premise is bizarre, and the letter is organized according to what Dr. Smith calls the six senses: sight, hearing, smelling, feeling, taste, and a sense he labels "psychic impression."

Smith writes to the US State Department and "resigns" from his role as a breeder. Dr. Smith pastes paper over his cell's windows in an attempt to prevent the State Department from "doping him."

Minnie arranges a lunacy trial for her son, and Dr. Smith is found *non compos mentis*, eliminating the need for a criminal proceeding. He is sentenced to the Mississippi State Insane Hospital. From this point forward, there is no record of Dr. Smith either confessing fault or proclaiming innocence of any crime. The question of his guilt in the rape case is never resolved.

The day before he is due to be transported to the hospital, Dr. Smith hides outside of his cell, which the jailer locked, assuming he was inside. At night, he flees on foot and disappears without a trace. Attempts to locate him by the local authorities are unsuccessful.

1925 Three weeks later, Dr. Smith resurfaces at the White House and gains audience with President Calvin Coolidge. He begins their conversation by describing plots against him by his many persecutors. The president quickly becomes aware of Smith's delusion and has him detained. The *Vicksburg Post* relates the incident in a story that month; this is the last contemporaneous recording of Dr. Smith suffering from delusions.

Nearly a month after Dr. Smith's escape, the sheriff of Claiborne County, Mississippi, retrieves Dr. Smith from detention in Washington, DC. He is brought to the Mississippi State Insane Hospital and admitted.

circa 1920s The Mississippi State Insane Hospital, originally built in the nineteenth century for a fraction of its current population, is overcrowded and decrepit.

1925 Daisy and Gerard Brandon arrive in Shreveport, where their daughter Ethel, alone with four children since Dr. Smith's departure, has been eking out a meager existence. Gerard announces they are all moving to Natchez.

In Natchez, Ethel and Daisy share day-to-day parenting duties while Gerard serves the role of father and head of household. Dr. Smith's name is never spoken. Margaret is told her father "had a fugue" and lost his way.

circa 1926 Understanding her father to be lost and searching for his way home, Margaret sits on the curb daily awaiting his arrival. One afternoon she is caught staring at the photograph of Dr. Smith that sits on the parlor mantle. The next day, the photograph disappears.

1926 Dr. Smith requests and is granted permission to visit his mother in Vicksburg. While there, he telegrams the hospital superintendent for permission to travel west. Denied, he still attempts to leave by train but is detained at the station and returned to the hospital.

1935 The original asylum closes and a new Mississippi State Hospital opens at Whitfield. The modern facility incorporates hydrotherapy, electroshock treatment, and medication in patient-focused treatment with the goal of remission. Dr. Smith and all remaining patients at the Old Asylum are transferred (with their medical records) to the new hospital.

circa 1935–1940s Relative to the Old Asylum, Whitfield is peaceful and spacious, boasting a beautiful campus. Dr. Smith purportedly joins the groundskeeping crew.

1942 Immediately prior to David Jr.'s WWII deployment, he visits his father at Whitfield. Dr. Smith, who had not seen his son since infancy, said, "I told Ethel to tell everyone I was dead. I don't want visitors." No other family members are known to have visited Dr. Smith during the entirety of his forty-year hospitalization.

circa 1940s–2010s A photograph of Dr. Smith sits in plain view on his daughter Margaret's desk. On the rare occasions someone asks about her father, she freezes, unable to respond.

1950 Dr. Smith is photographed for a Jackson newspaper article on the occupational therapy program at Whitfield. The photo shows a bearded and visored man seated at a loom; its caption indicates he is making curtains and bedspreads.

circa 1950s–1960s Whitfield is largely self-sufficient, with patients farming, cooking, and tending livestock for the facility. Smith is offered release on multiple occasions but declines each time.

1963 Anna Virginia Wesley (Dr. Smith's granddaughter, Margaret's daughter, and Noah Saterstrom's mother) matriculates at Millsaps College. The Jackson campus is just a few hundred yards from the site of the Old Asylum and only ten miles from Whitfield, which is still Dr. Smith's home. Anna, unaware of his hospitalization and believing him dead, never meets her grandfather.

1965 Dr. Smith dies at Whitfield, having spent forty years committed—at first forcibly, and then, at some unknown point, voluntarily. Records of his diagnosis, treatment, and apparent recovery are moved to a third-party storage site and become lost to time and bureaucracy. Dr. Smith is believed to be buried at Whitfield, in one of Rose Hill Cemetery's graves whose markers have disappeared or been damaged over time.

2014 On March 13, Margaret Gerard Smith Wesley dies. She never spoke of her father, only saying, when pressed, "He was an optometrist."

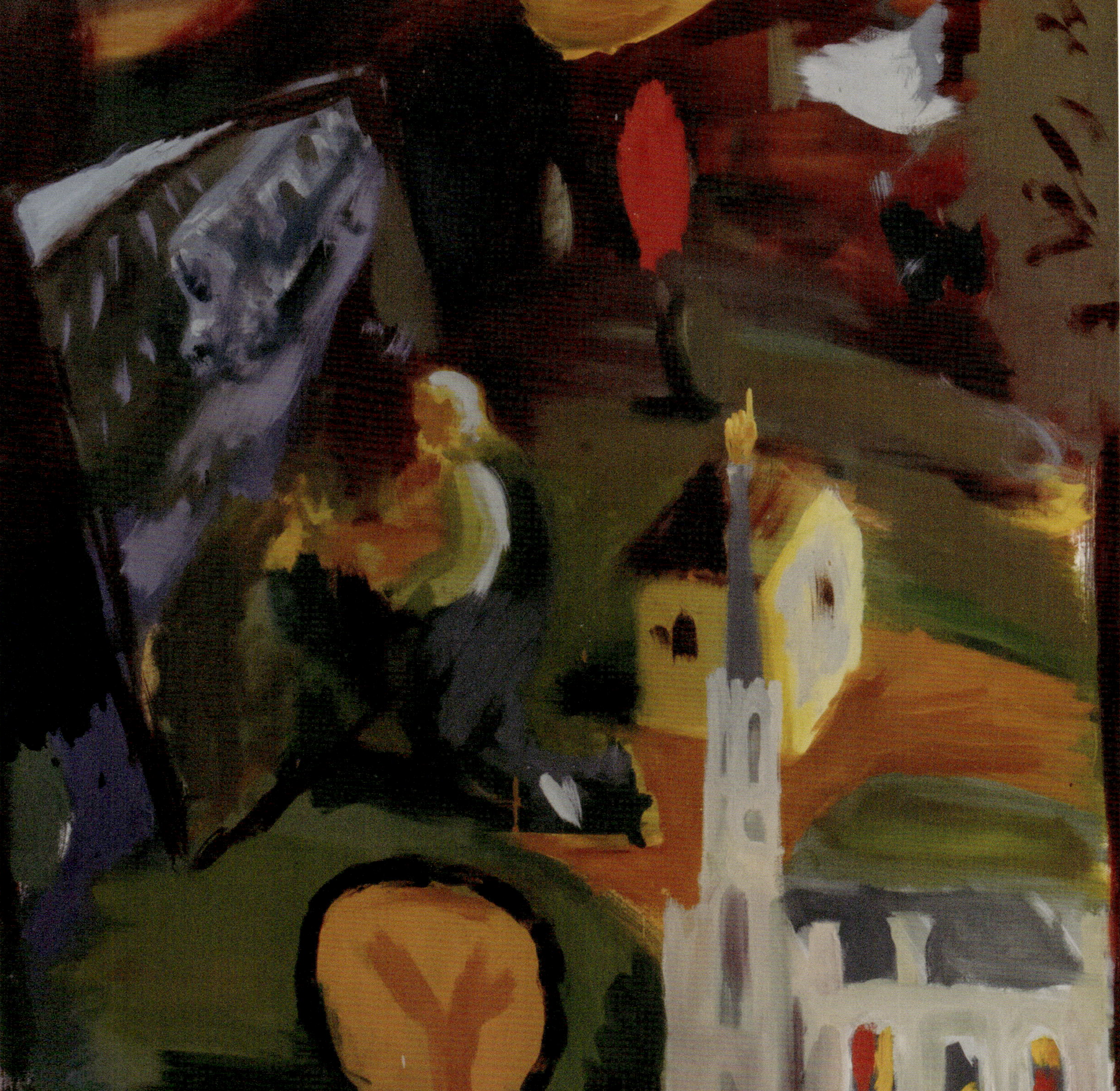

A SELECTION OF

SATERSTROM'S FAMILY

ARCHIVES

DR. D. L. SMITH

OPTOMETRIST

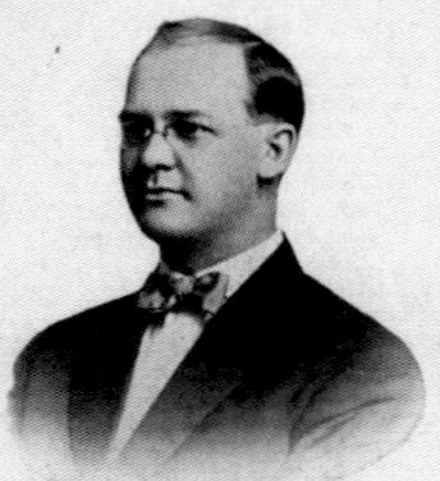

OFFICE, DASTE'S DRUG STORE
2925 BAYOU ROAD

RESIDENCE, 1437 N. MIRO ST.

NEW ORLEANS, LA.

AT THE COMMERCIAL
→HOTEL←

GLASSES AND HEALTH

THE value of perfectly fitted glasses with reference to health cannot be overestimated. The effect upon the nervous system is direct upon the entire organism.

The nerves constitute the most wonderful telegraphic system imaginable, with direct wires from the brain to all parts of the anatomy. This system is divided into three distinct classes—viz.: Motor Nerves, which control all muscular action; Nerves of Sensation, which inform us promptly of any accident or derangement of any part of the system; Nerves of Special Sense, which enable us to see, hear, feel, smell and taste.

The stomach is the galvanic battery which, through its functions of digestion, generates the electricity which supplies the nerves with the vital energy necessary to enable them to perform their duties. Electricity is also generated by the lungs and the atoms of our bodies.

This electric force is manufactured and stored in the brain, so that, in case the stomach becomes disordered and fails to perform its work, the reserve may be drawn upon while the damage is being repaired. The connections with this reservoir are so arranged that an equitable distribution of force may be afforded its various patrons. If, by reason of a lack of natural development, one of these patrons finds it necessary to draw more than its share of the daily supply manufactured, the excess must come from the reserve, and it follows that it is only a matter of time until the reservoir is drained and trouble begins.

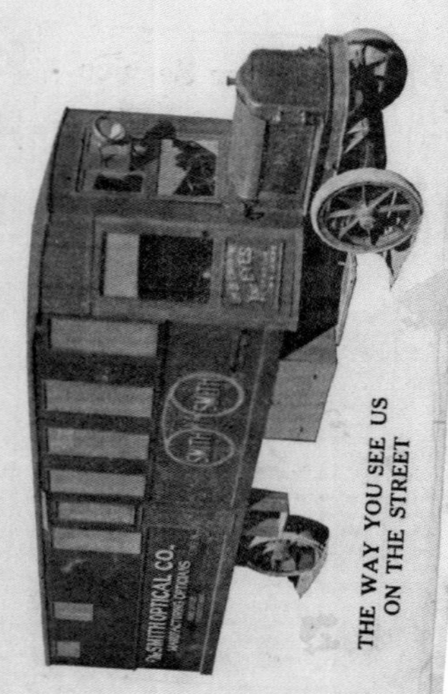

THE WAY YOU SEE US ON THE STREET

What Our Service Means to You

IN BRIEF OUR SERVICE means the placing in your town at regular intervals an OPTICAL EQUIPMENT for examining your eyes, grinding glasses and taking care of your repairs, equal in capacity to the average high class city optical office.

In the past it has been necessary for citizens of these towns to purchase glazed glasses from merchandise stores, etc., or from traveling opticians, (some of whom are very incompetent) or, at the best, to incur the expense of going to the nearest city to have their eyes examined, their glasses being mailed to them after their return home which deprives them of the opportunity of an immediate adjustment should any part of the filling of the prescription be in error.

The inventor of the portable optical shop has appreciated for a long time the need of a service that would eliminate these inconveniences but was required to devote years of work to designing special optical equipment which made it possible to congest in so small a space the service we now present to you.

It is reasonable to assume that the vast amount of inside information which our investors possess places us in a better position than even you yourself to judge who is competent to examine your eyes, and the very liberal guarantee which you receive from us follows:

"THE SMITH OPTICAL CO., (not incorporated) of Vicksburg, Miss., guarantees your glasses to be as represented, free from defects in material and workmanship and that we will replace these lenses at any time within one year should they fail to give entire satisfaction, or refund not more than seventy five per cent of the total price received, provided complaint is made within thirty days."

This guarantee is worthy of your consideration, and we hope that should your eyes trouble you that you will take advantage of our service, we are.

The Smith Optical Company
VICKSBURG, MISSISSIPPI

Our examiner will call at your home and examine your eyes when requested to do so.

GLASSES FITTED
FROM $5.00
AND UP

First Quality Stock Only
No Seconds Used

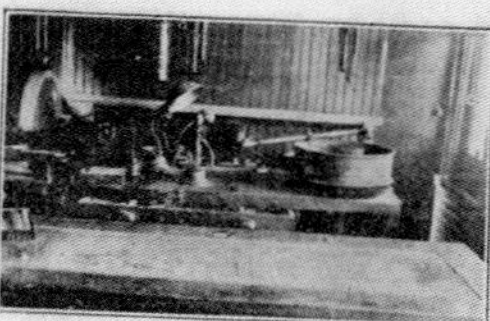

View of Part of Shop Where Your Glasses are Ground. Contained Within the Truck.

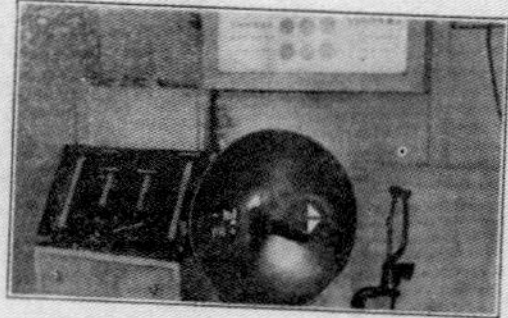

View of Part of Examination Room Where Your Eyes are Examined. Contained Within the Truck.

Headaches, pain on top of head, pain in back of neck, inflamed eyes, granulated lids, eyes watering, fluttering eyes, reading running together, seeing two objects at once, cross-eyes, bright specks and dark specks, balls of fire, a scum or curtain formed before the eyes, nervous indigestion of the stomach, fluttering of the heart, numb, prickling feeling in hands and arms, sick stomach, nervous prostration, insomnia—these troubles all come from the result of eye strain.

Don't think because you can see that you are not in need of glasses. It is a common occurrence for people to say, "If I quit reading for a little while and look away into space, I experience relief and can work for some time afterwards with comparative comfort." This is because the few moments of rest have allowed a little nerve force to accumulate, and when this is exhausted another rest must be resorted to.

It is not unreasonable to assert that a very large per cent. of nervous diseases may be absolutely cured without the aid of medicine other than a pair of properly fitted glasses.

As muscular functions of life itself are dependent upon a sufficient amount of nerve force, the mind, the most delicate of attributes of the human body, requires perfect nerve connections, and it is the first to note and be distressed at a shortage. More nervous disorders come from this than all other causes combined.

Now, I don't wish to say that I can cure these troubles with just a pair of glasses, or that I will fit you a pair if you are under the care of a physician; but, if your physician has any reason to believe that they will help you, I guarantee to fit you correctly.

Think over your condition carefully, and if you think you can be benefited by glasses let me know and I will call, or you can come to me, examination free, and if you don't need them I will surely tell you truthfully.

TEST YOUR OWN EYES

WE KNOW BUT ONE THING

WE KNOW BUT ONE THING

ASTIGMATISM TEST

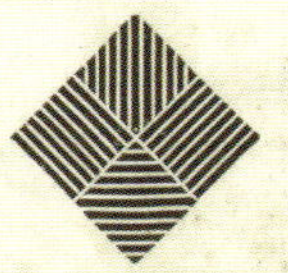

To make the astigmatism test, place the card at arm's length or further. Then notice the appearance of the blocks. If one or more appear blacker to you than the rest of them, you have astigmatism. You may check this by placing the card in different positions. You will see that the block with the lines running in the same direction as the one you first noted will now appear to be the blacker. If the blocks appear of equal blackness at all distances, there is no astigmatism present.

READING AND DISTANCE TEST

In 1906 William Campbell Posey, Professor of Ophthalmology in the Philadelphia Polyclinic, and William G. Spiller, Professor of Neuro-Pathology in the University of Pennsylvania, published a book on the eye and nervous system. This work expounded the experiences of the greatest authorities of the world. Under the heading, "Neurosis Occasioned By Eye Strain," they brought to light facts concerning the various disorders of the body as occasioned by the absence of properly fitted glasses. They give credit for the discovery that nervous disorders resulted from uncorrected optical errors to Dr. S. Weir Mitchell, who published two forcible articles on that subject,

one in The Medical and Surgical Reporter, 1874, and the other in The American Journal of Medical Sciences, 1876. Later, Dr. William Thompson, in 1879, contributed a paper to the Medical News Library on Astigmatism As the Cause of Headaches. He stated therein that more than ten years before he became aware that persons who consulted him

for defective eyesight presented symptoms which he enumerated as pain in the brow, temples, and occiput; as one of fullness in the head amounting to vertigo; nausea; insomnia; loss of appetite; fear of impending apoplexy; epilepsy; and general nervous prostration; chronic twitching or wrinkling

of the muscles of the forehead and face;—all of which he had seen relieved by correcting the optical error. Other Ophthalmic surgeons had also witnessed marked relief of headaches and other conditions as soon as glasses were worn. The rea-

sons that these disorders had not been traced to eye strain sooner was because generally the sufferer, if under forty-five years of age, will

HAVE PERFECT VISION. ALSO AT THAT TIME THE PROFESSION AS A WHOLE WERE NOT AS WELL INFORMED ABOUT THE PROPER FITTING OF GLASSES AS THEY ARE TODAY.

This Type should be read with comfort at from 10 to 14 inches.

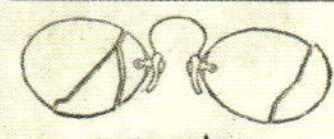

SAVE THE PIECES
BRING THEM TO THE
DR. SMITH OPTICAL COMPANY
AND GET NEW LENSES WITHIN ONE HOUR

This Type should be read at 8 feet and not further than 10 feet

THERE ARE 680,000 DIFFERENT COMBINATIONS OF LENSES USED IN FITTING GLASSES. WE KNOW THE CORRECT ONE FOR YOUR **EYES**

PHONE 670
VICKSBURG, MISS.

THE DOCTOR SMITH OPTICAL COMPANY

1419 WASHINGTON ST.
VICKSBURG, MISS.

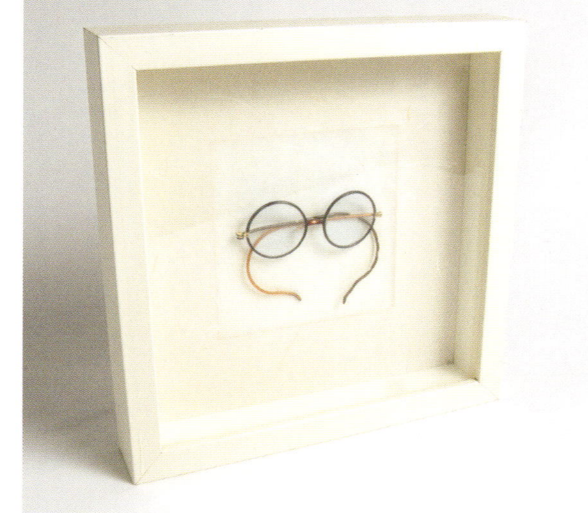

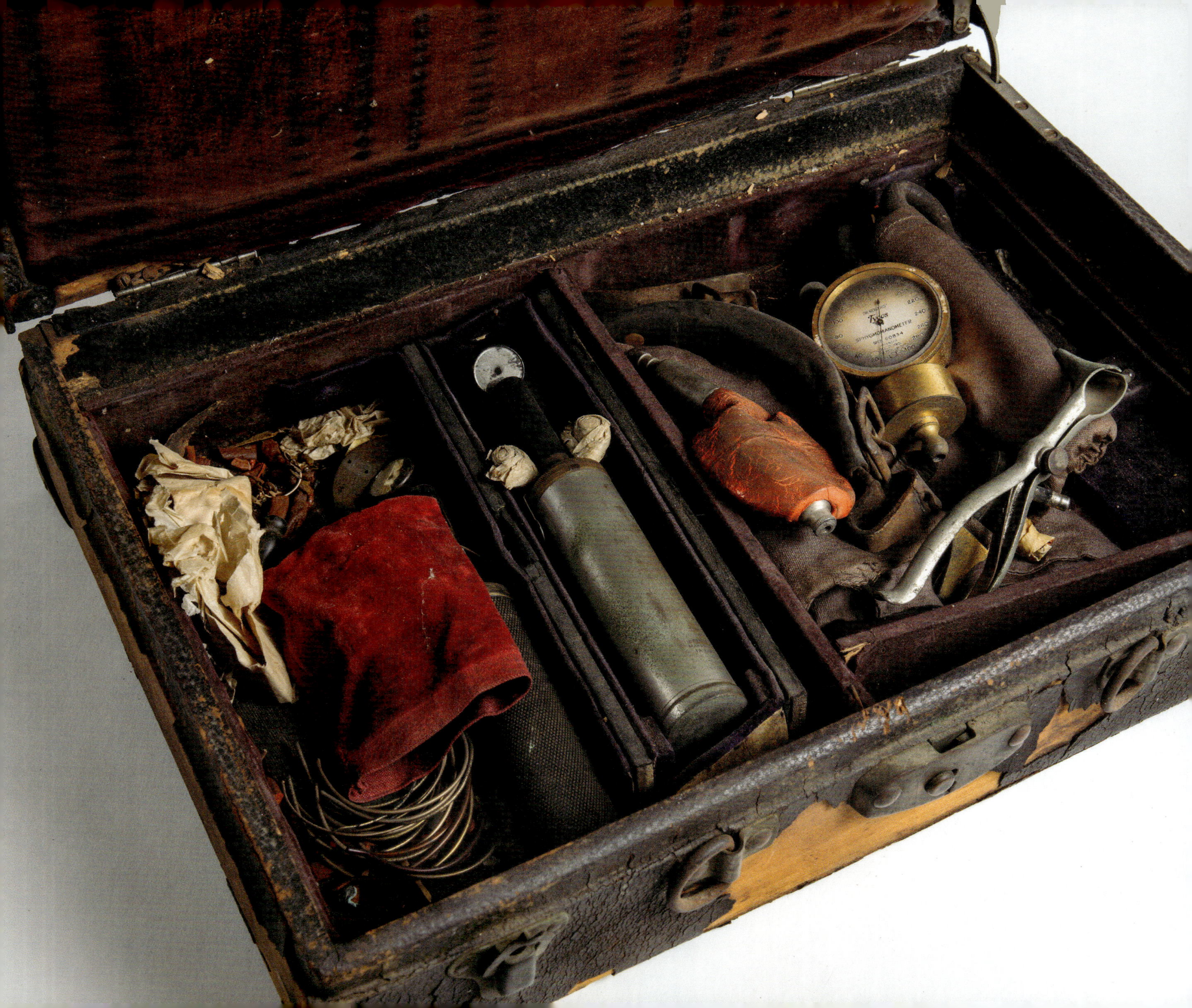
Tycos
SPHYGMOMANOMETER

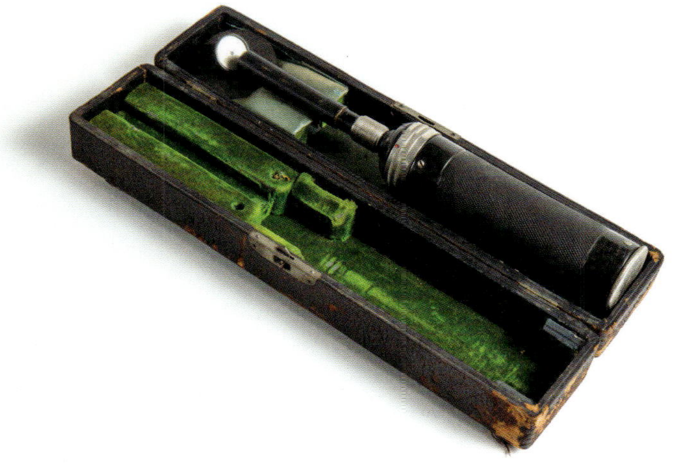

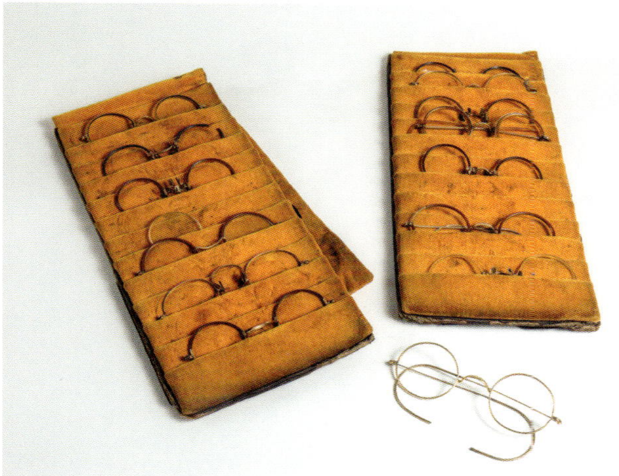

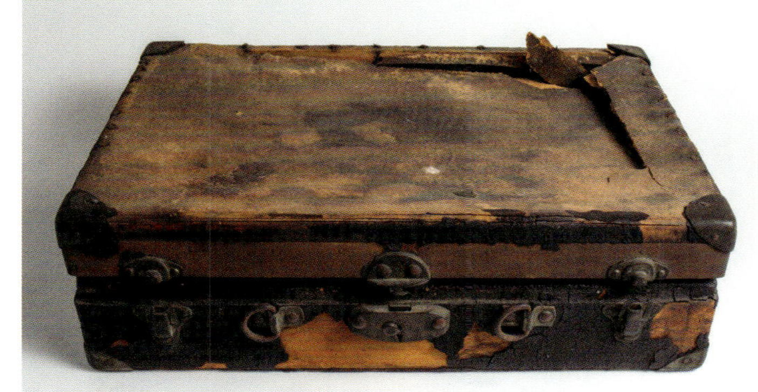

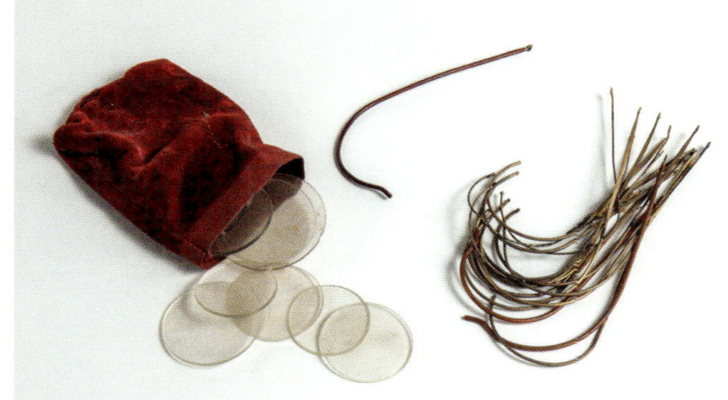

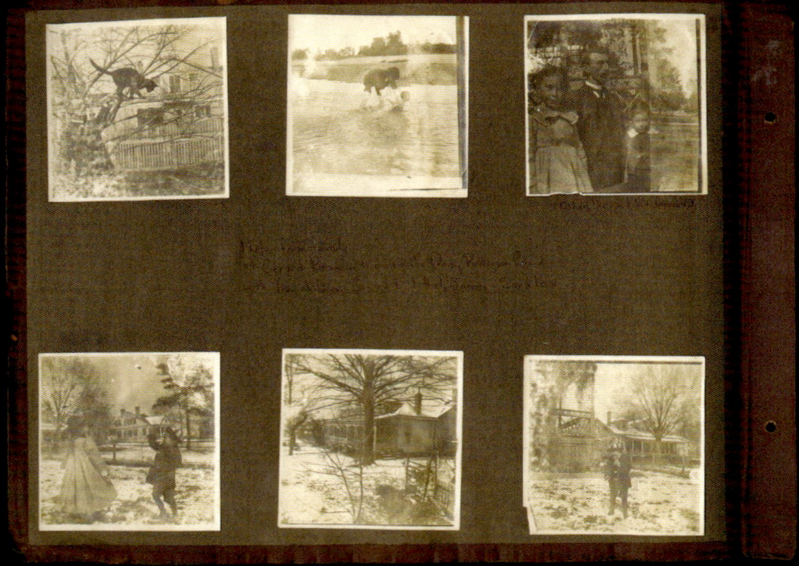

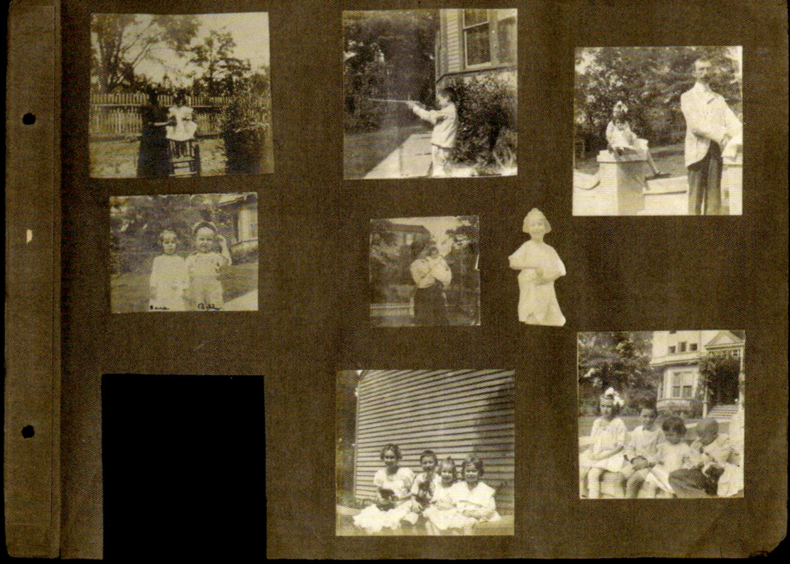

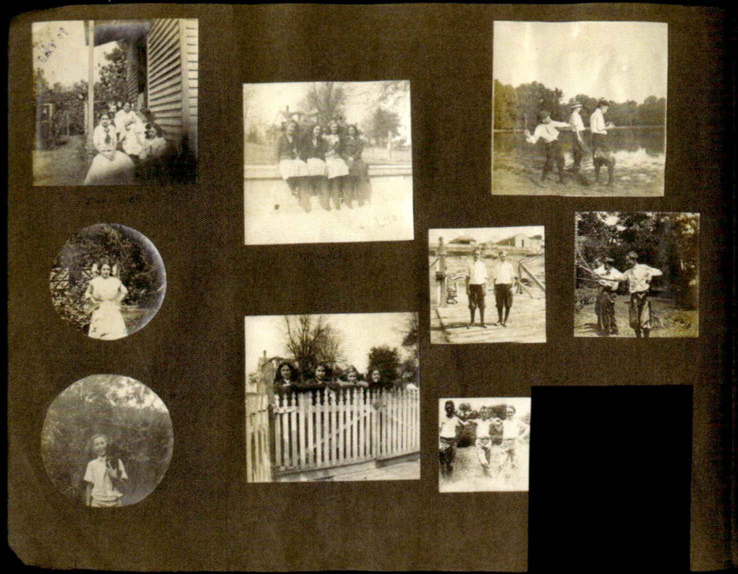

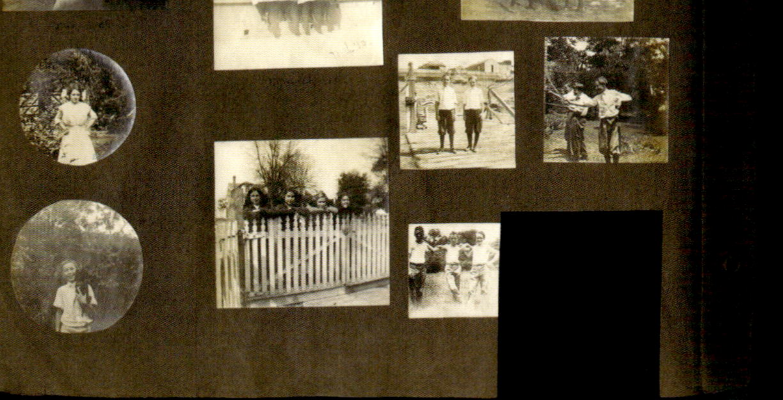

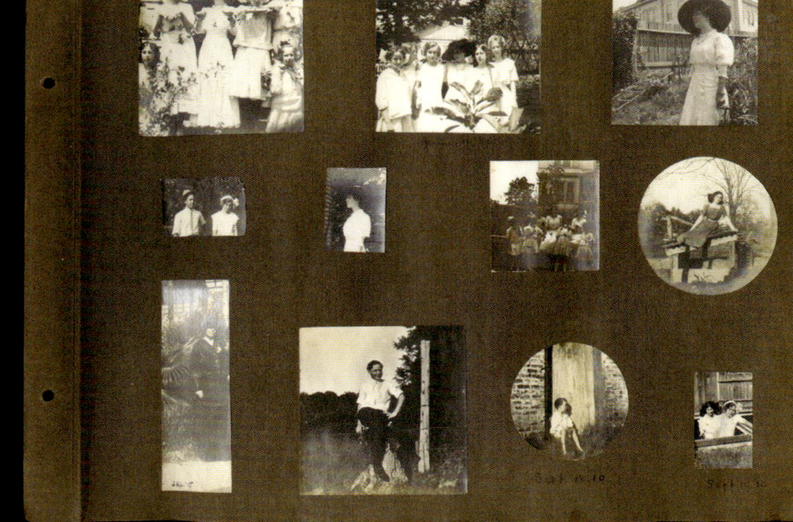

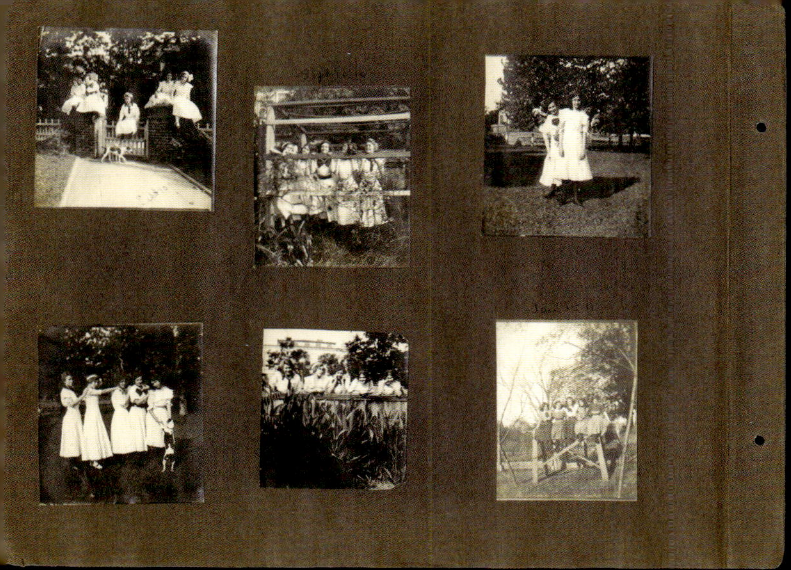

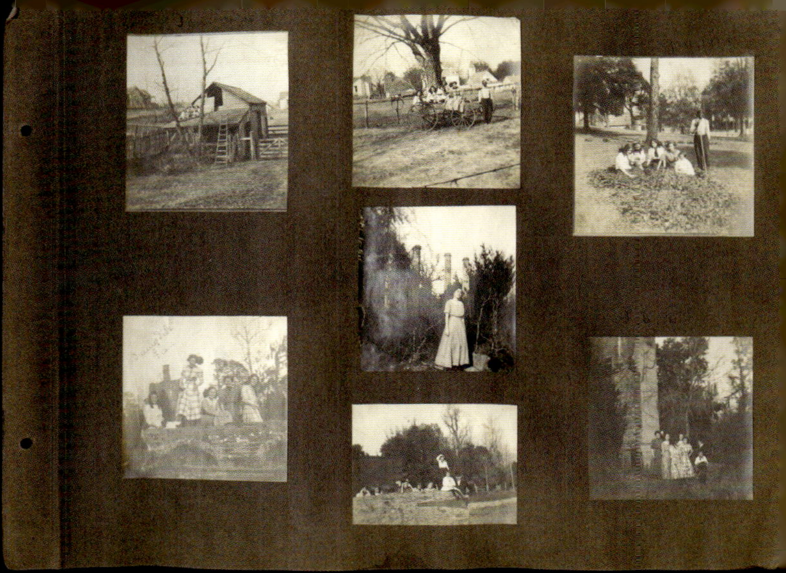

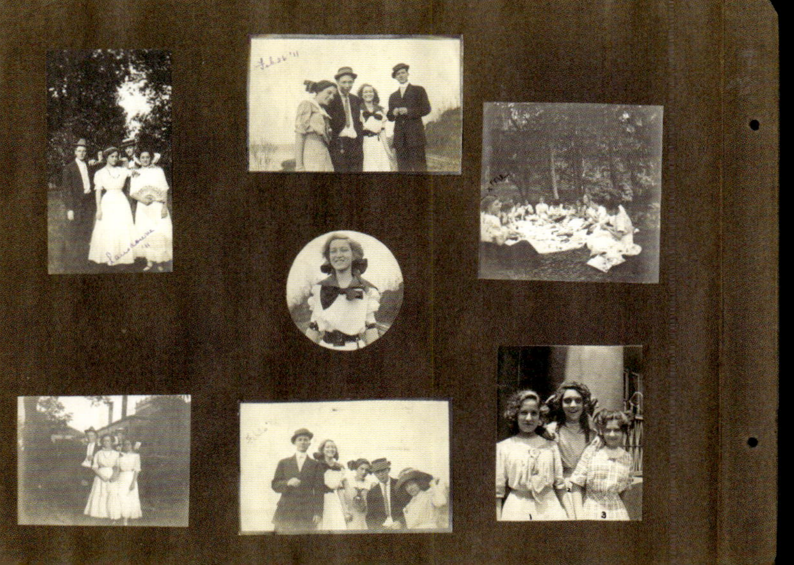

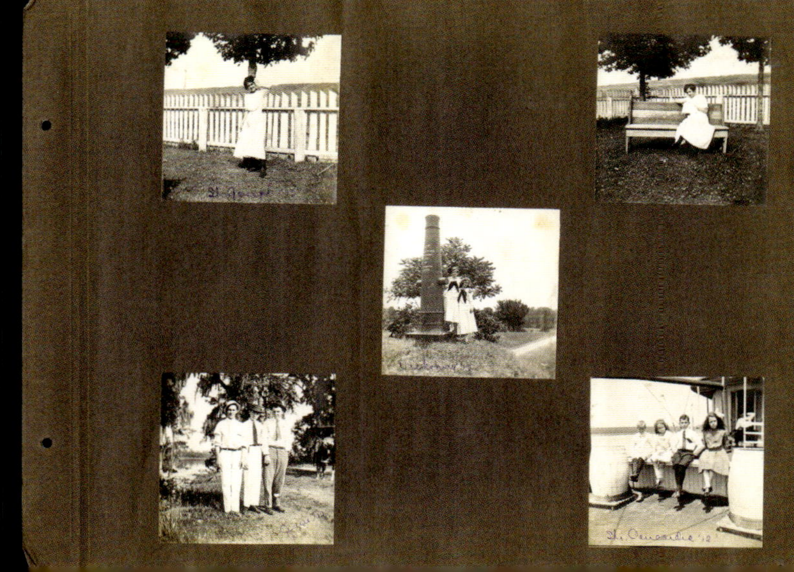

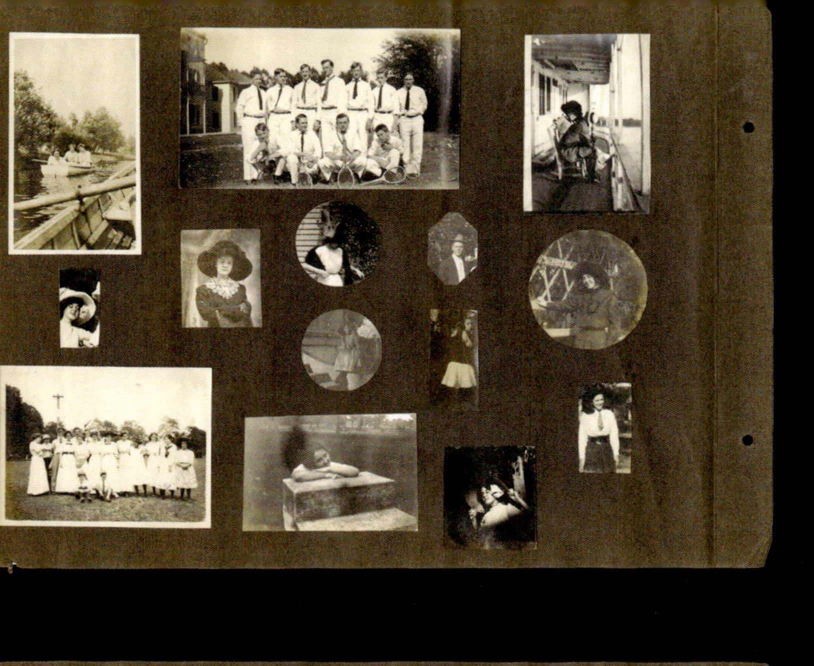
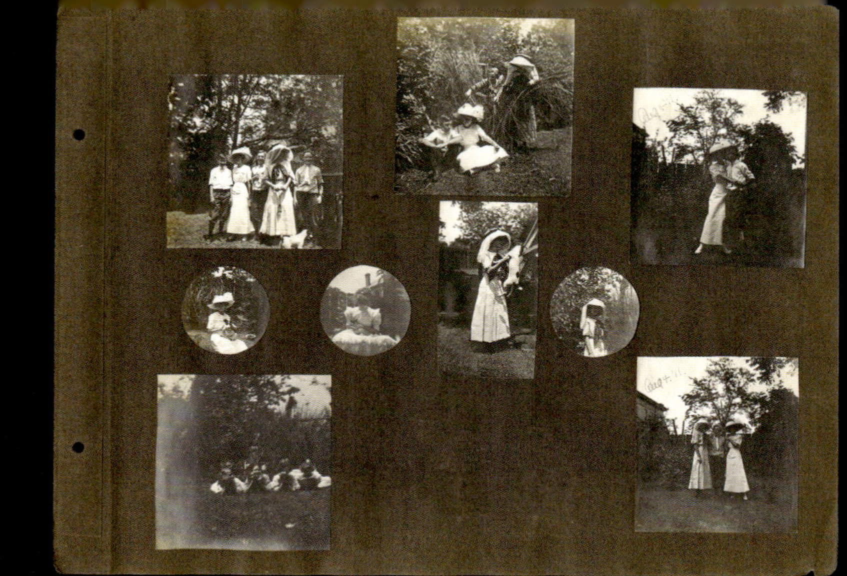
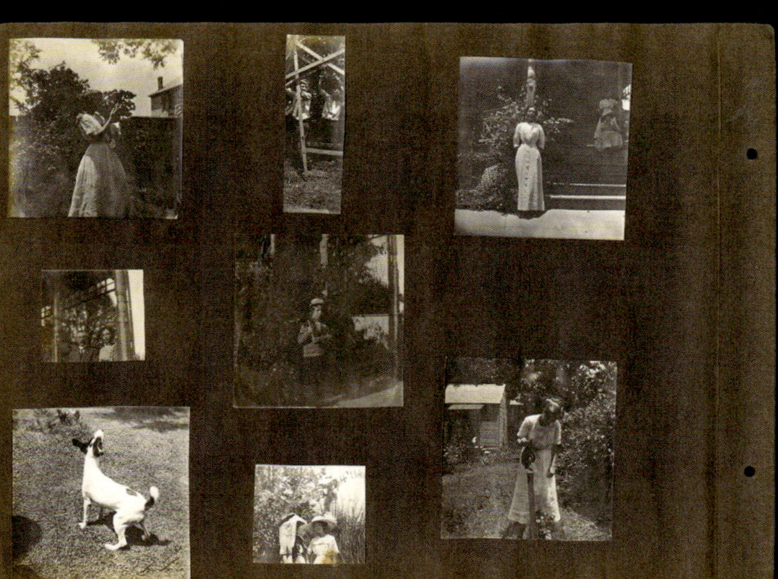
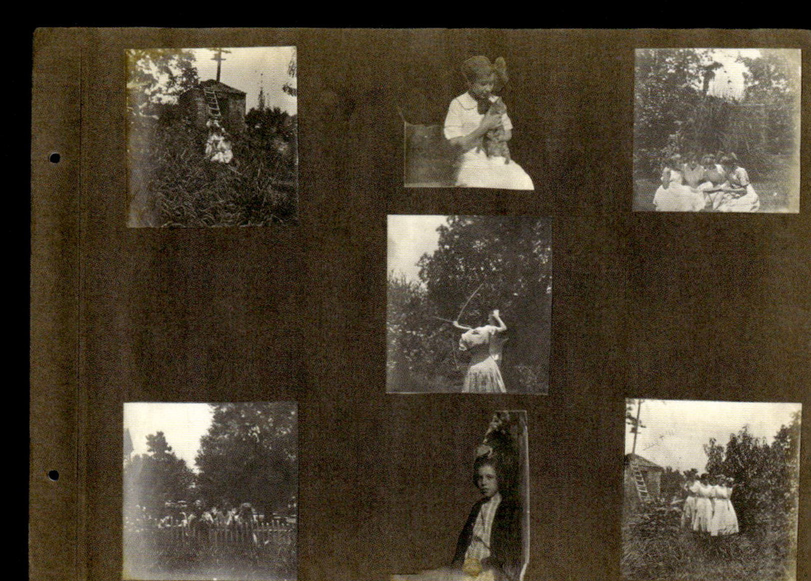

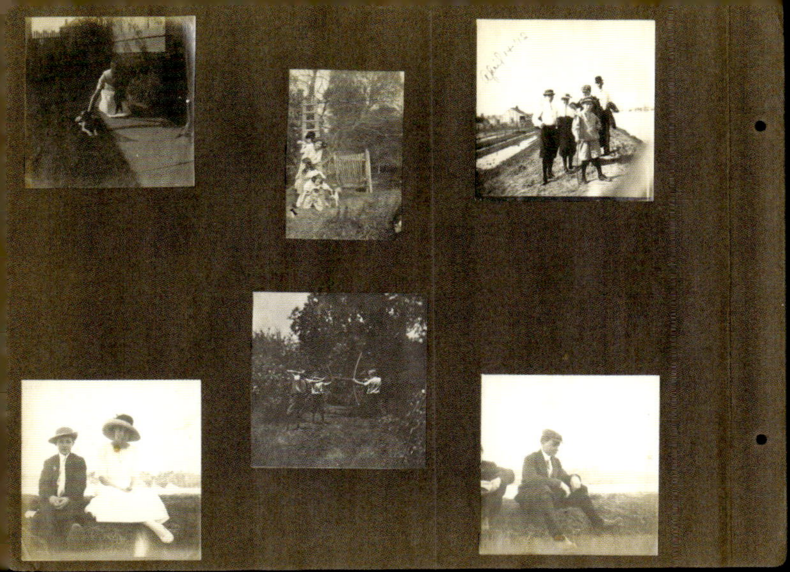

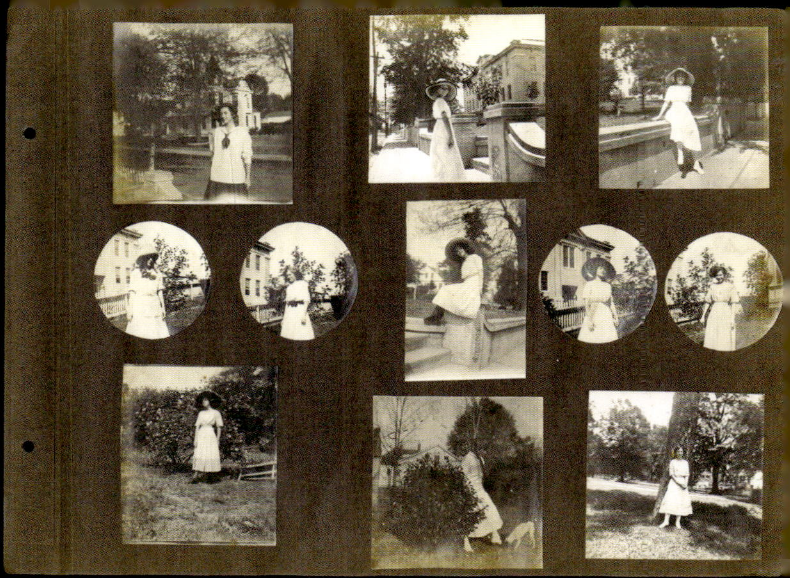

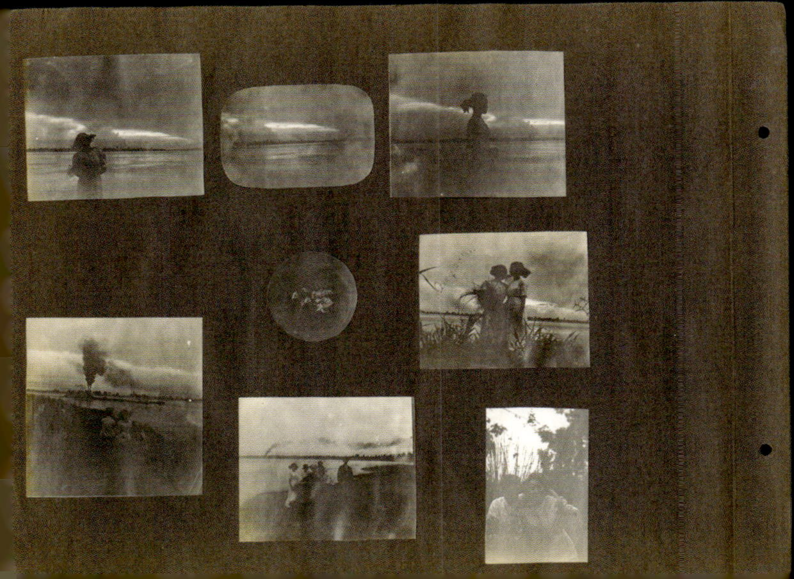

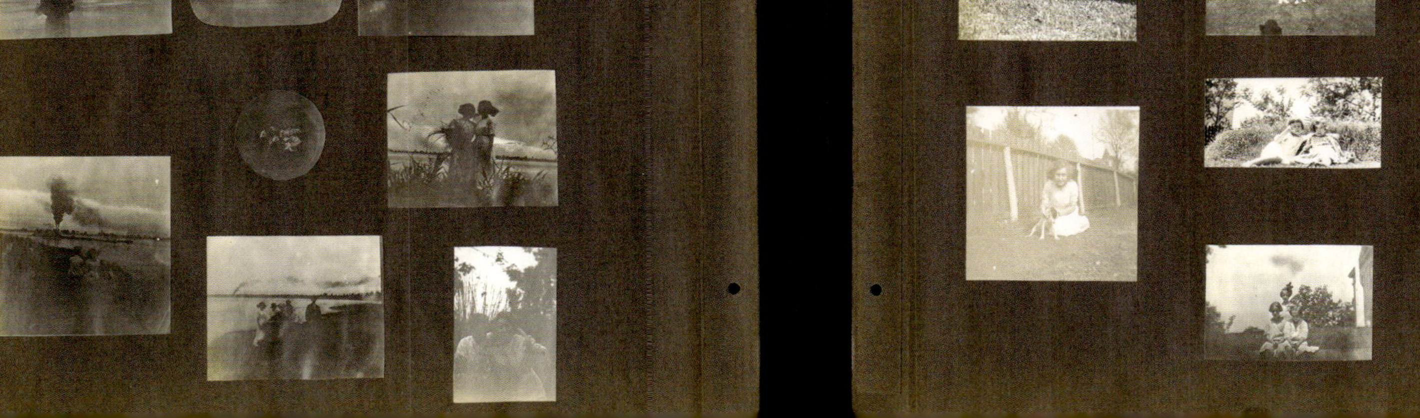

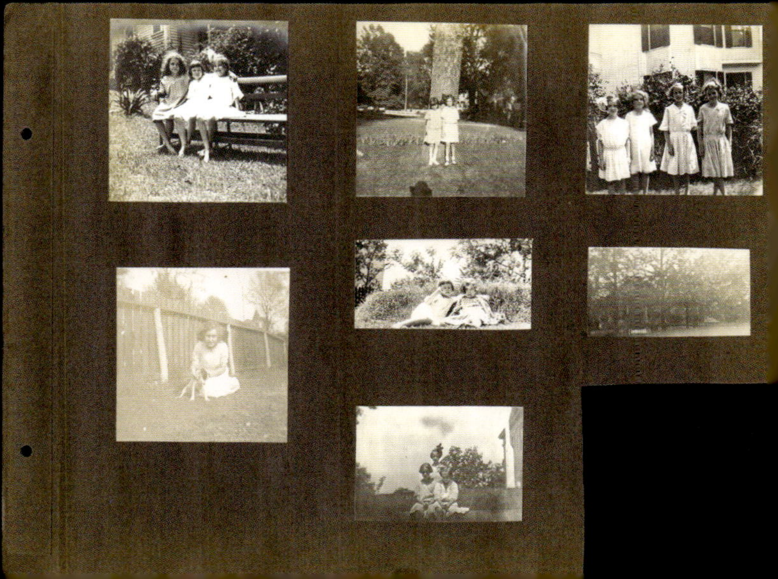

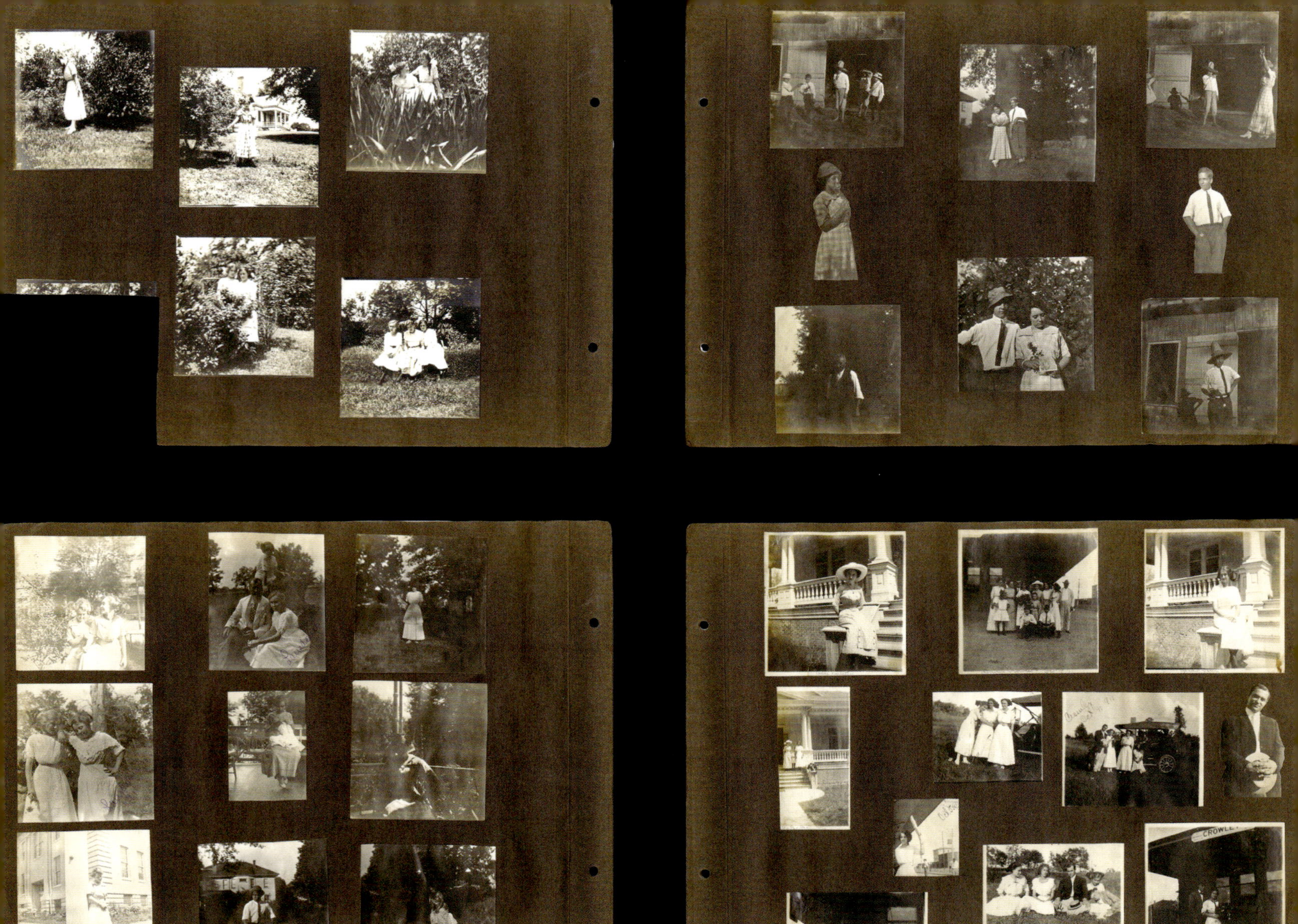

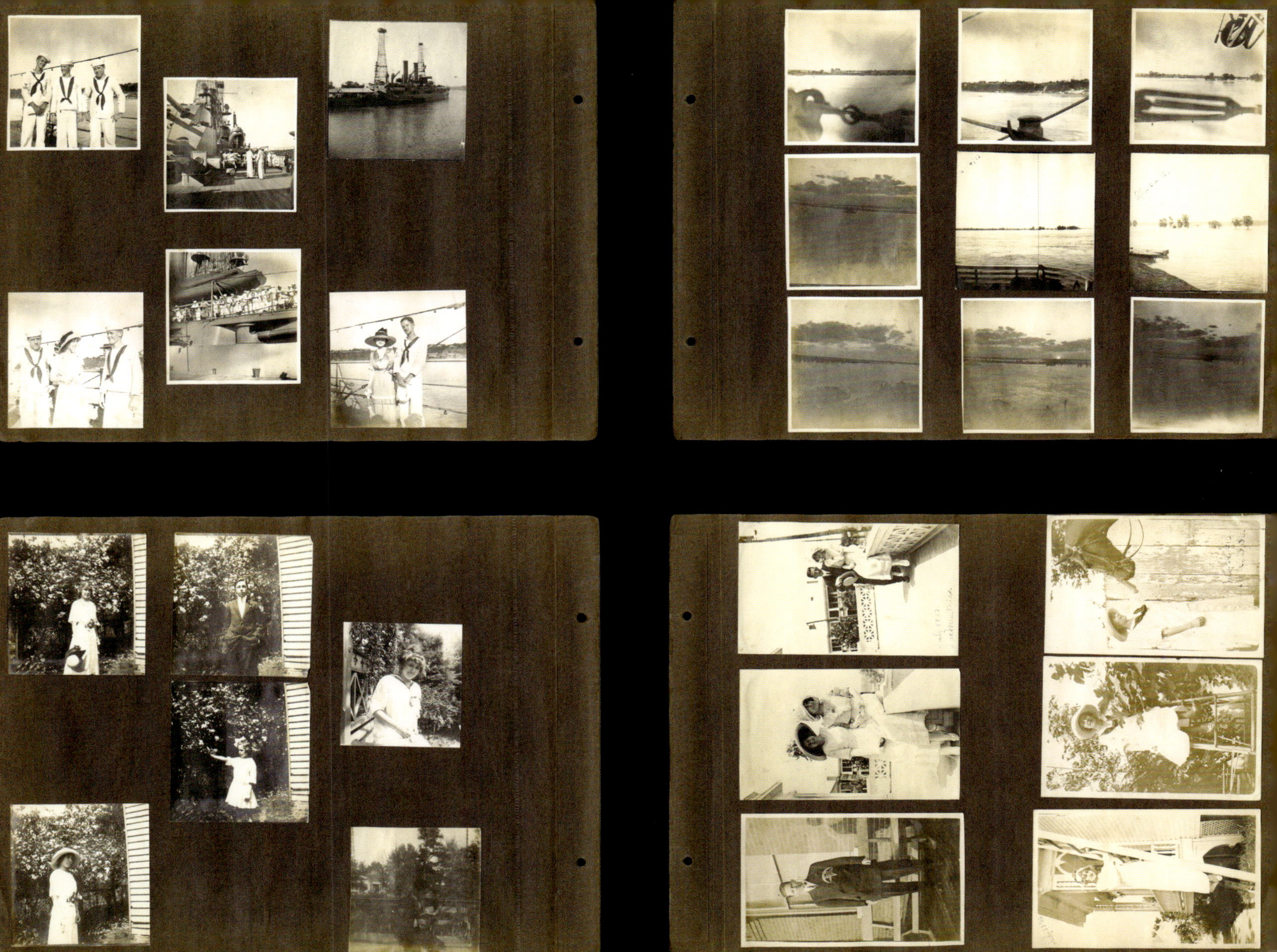

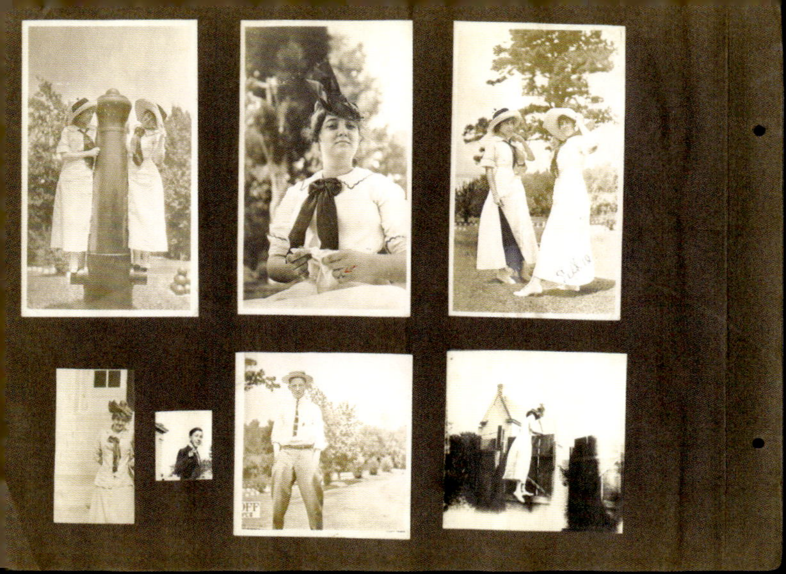

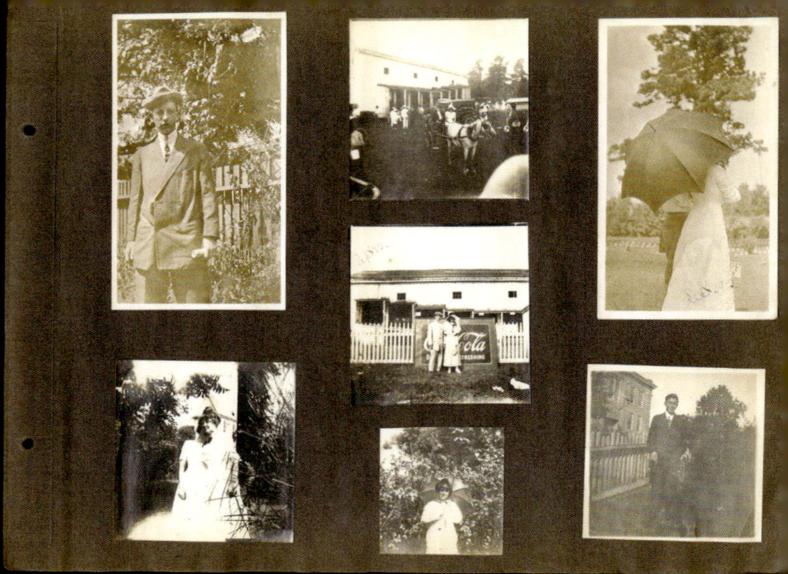

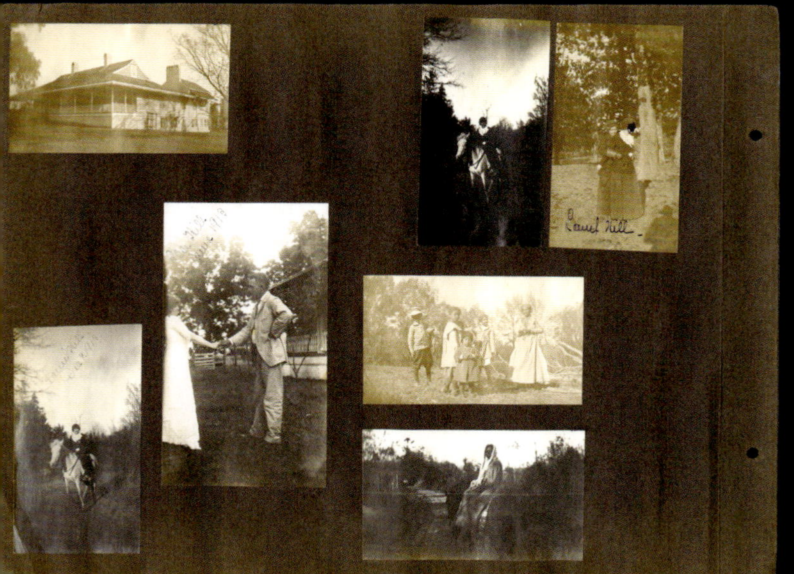

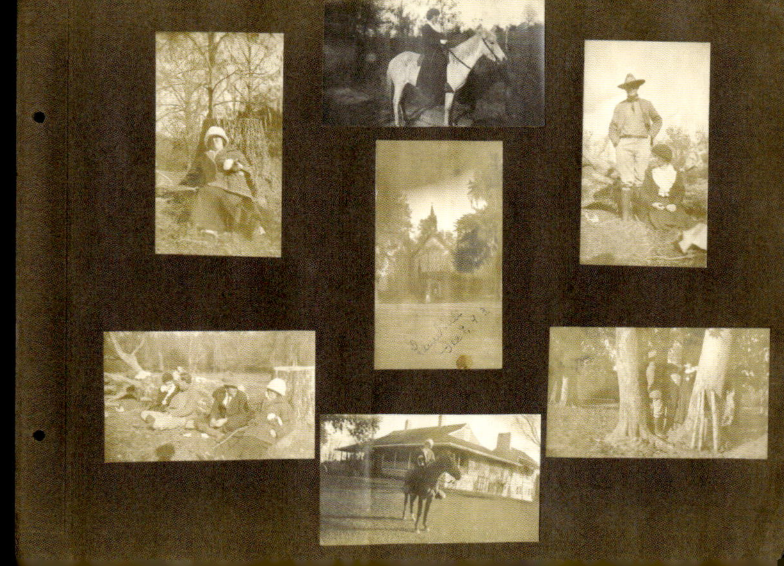

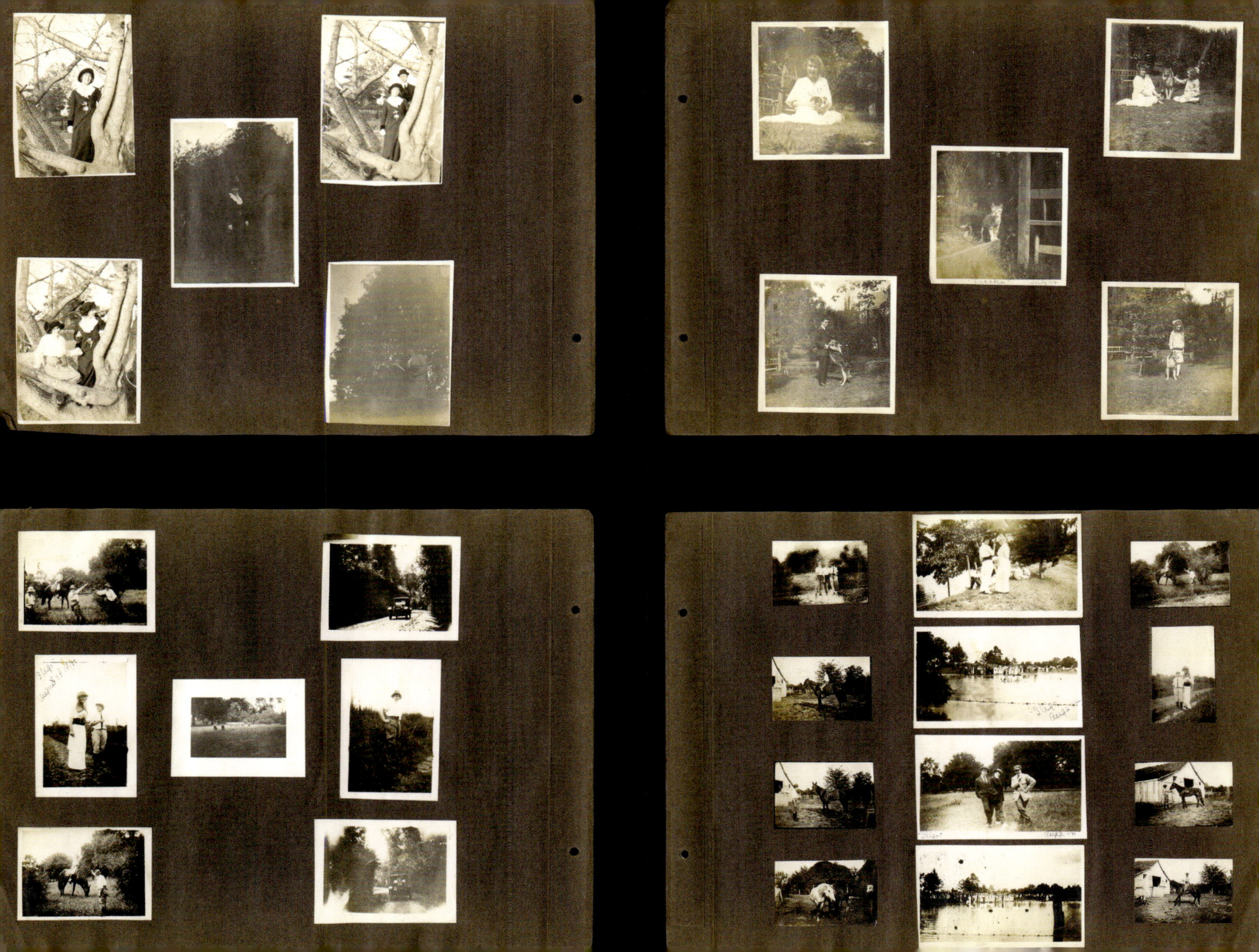

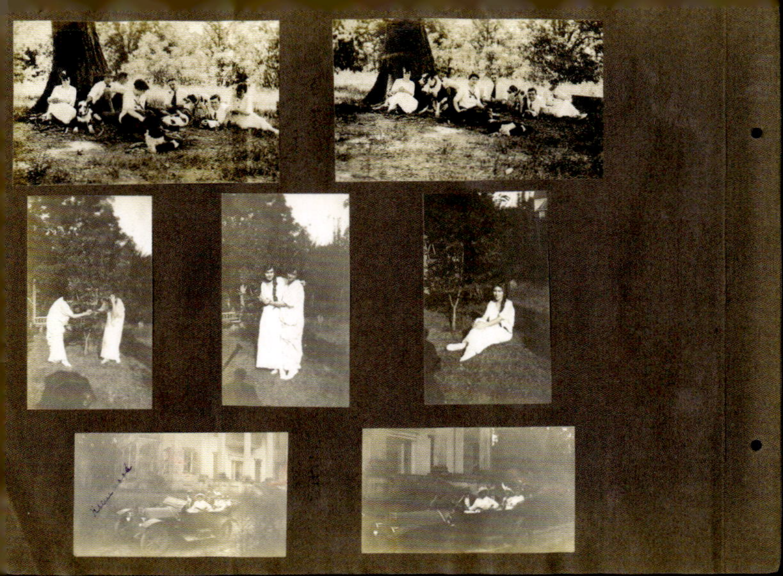

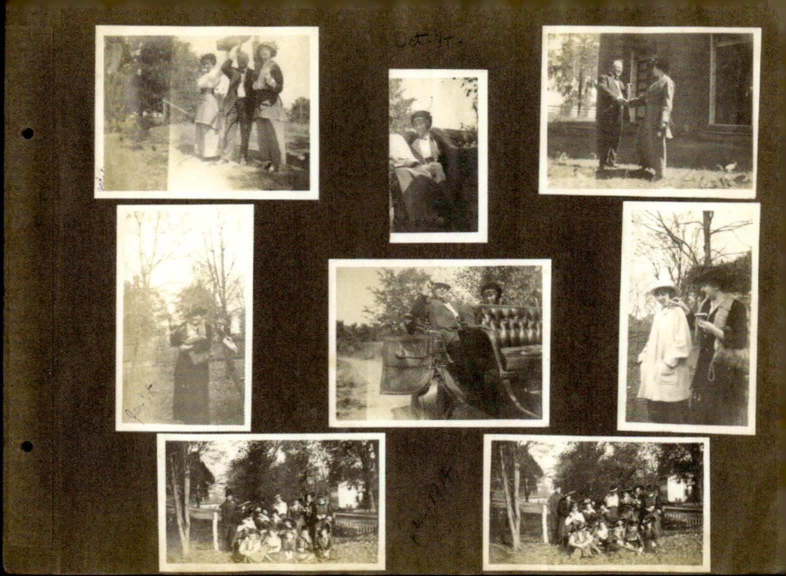

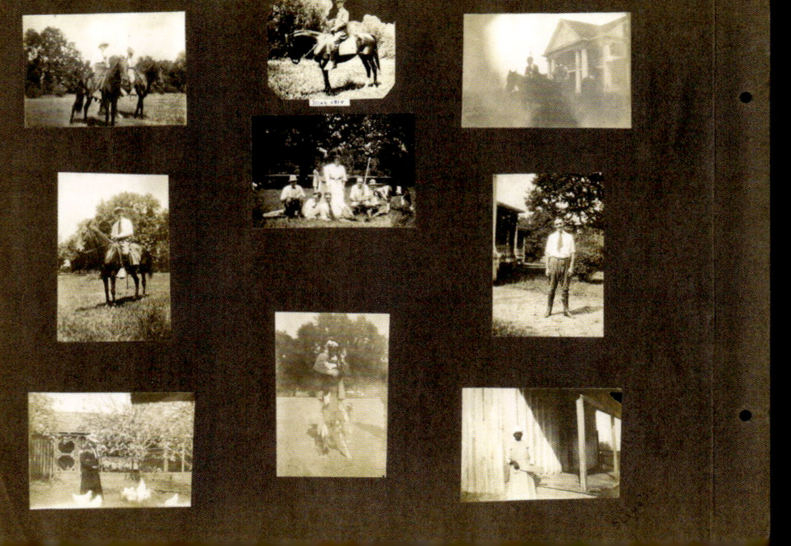

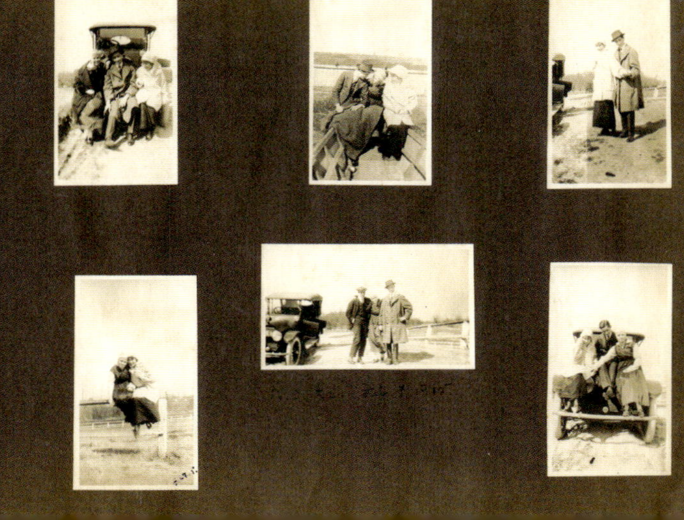

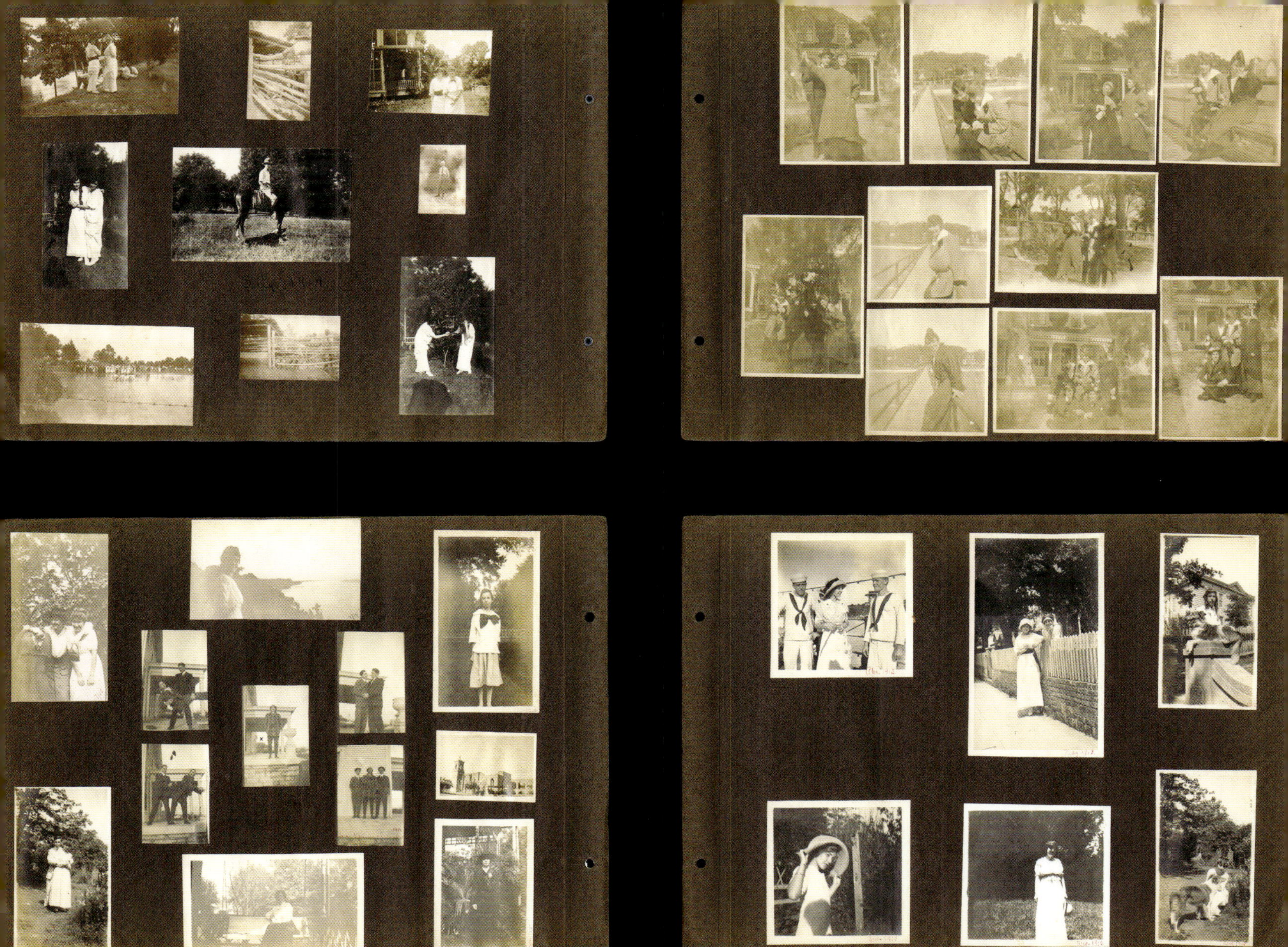

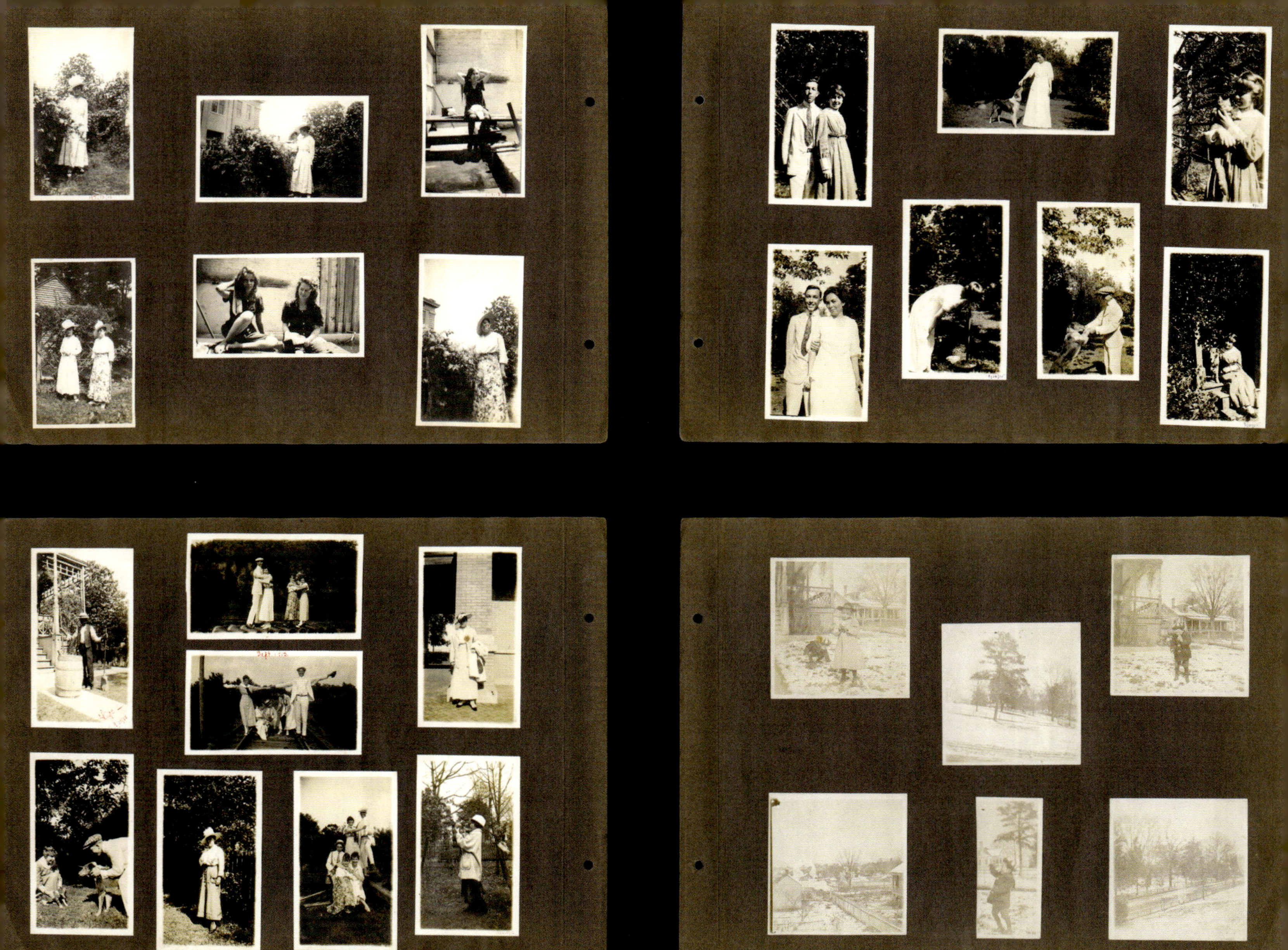

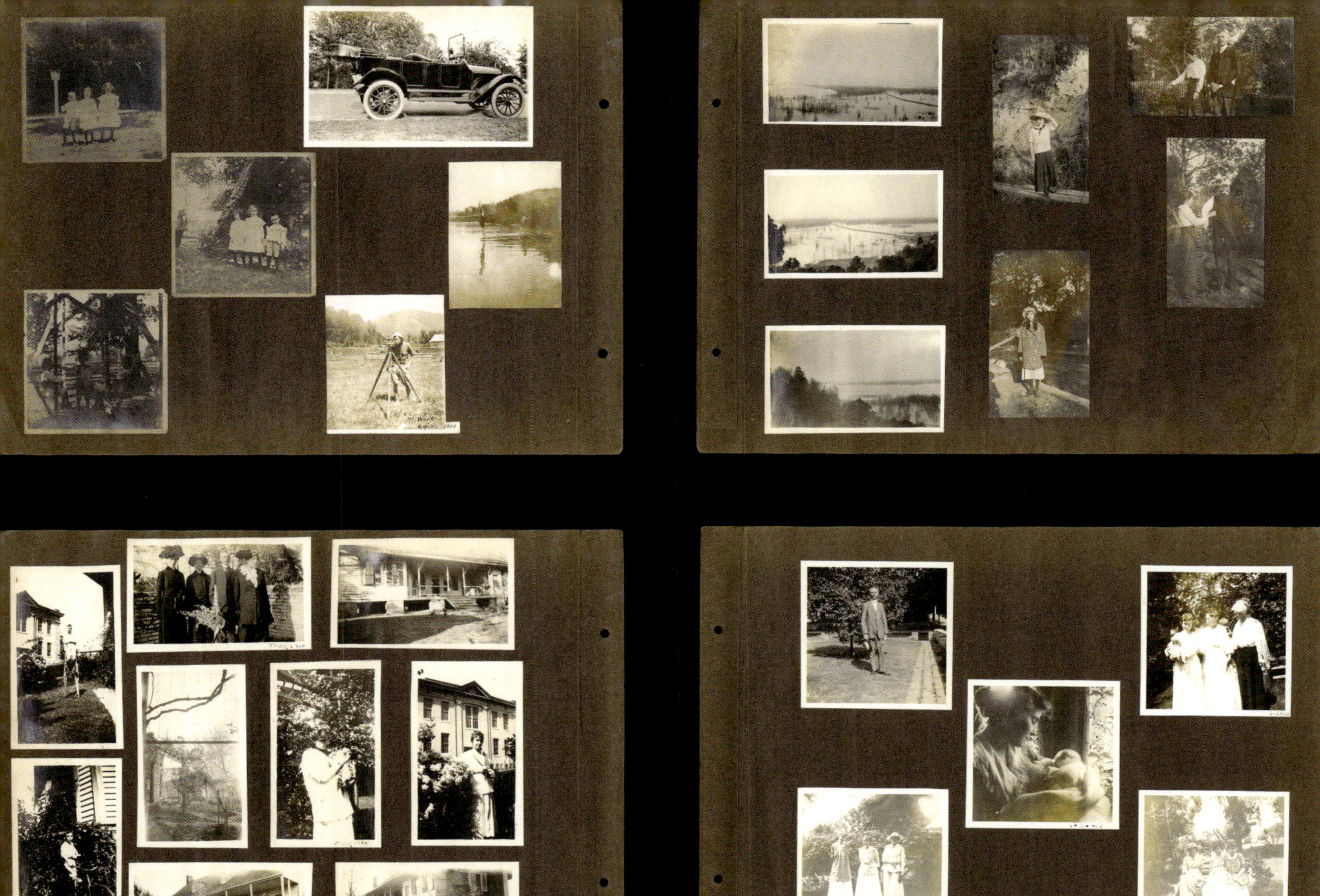

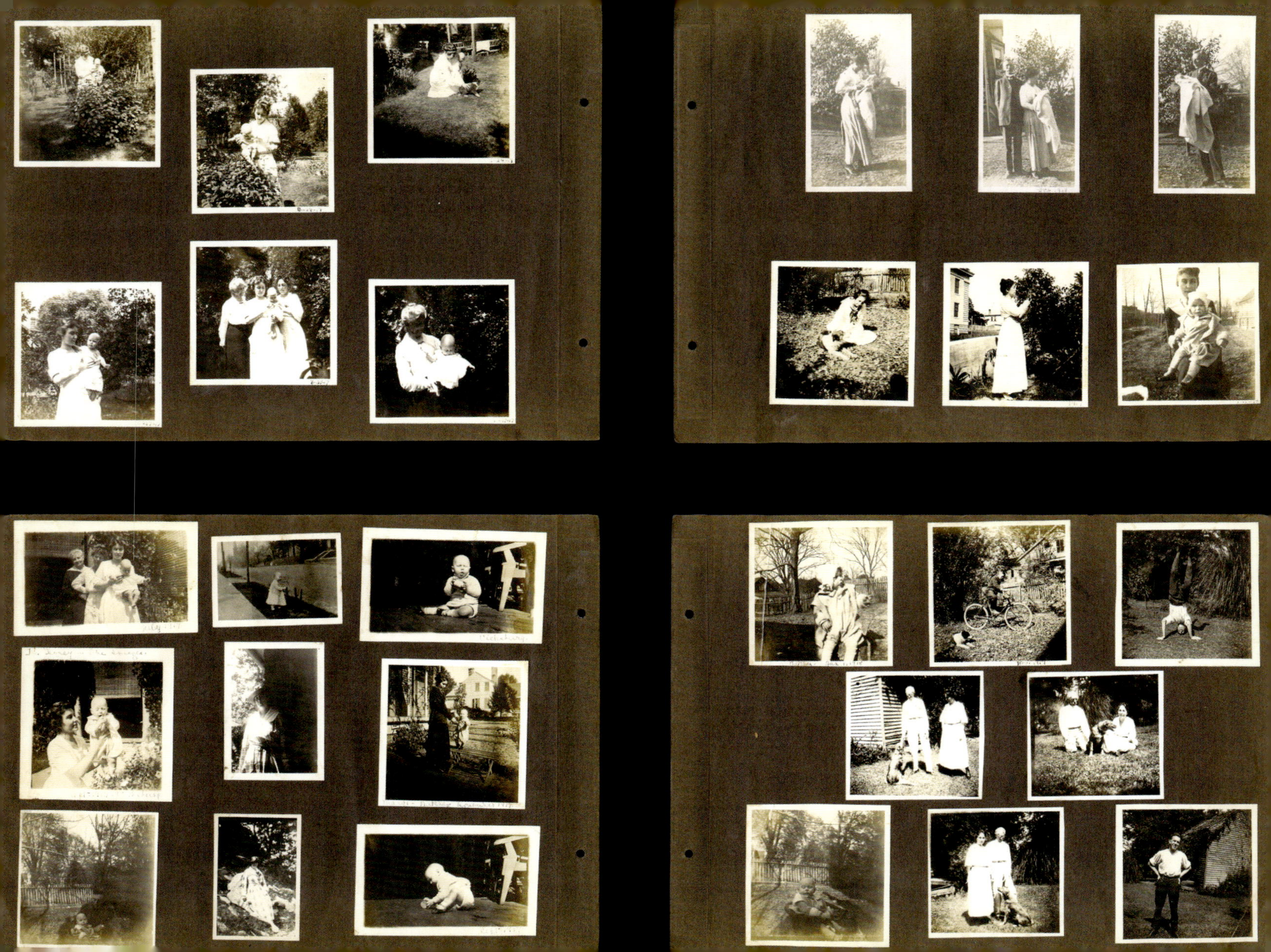

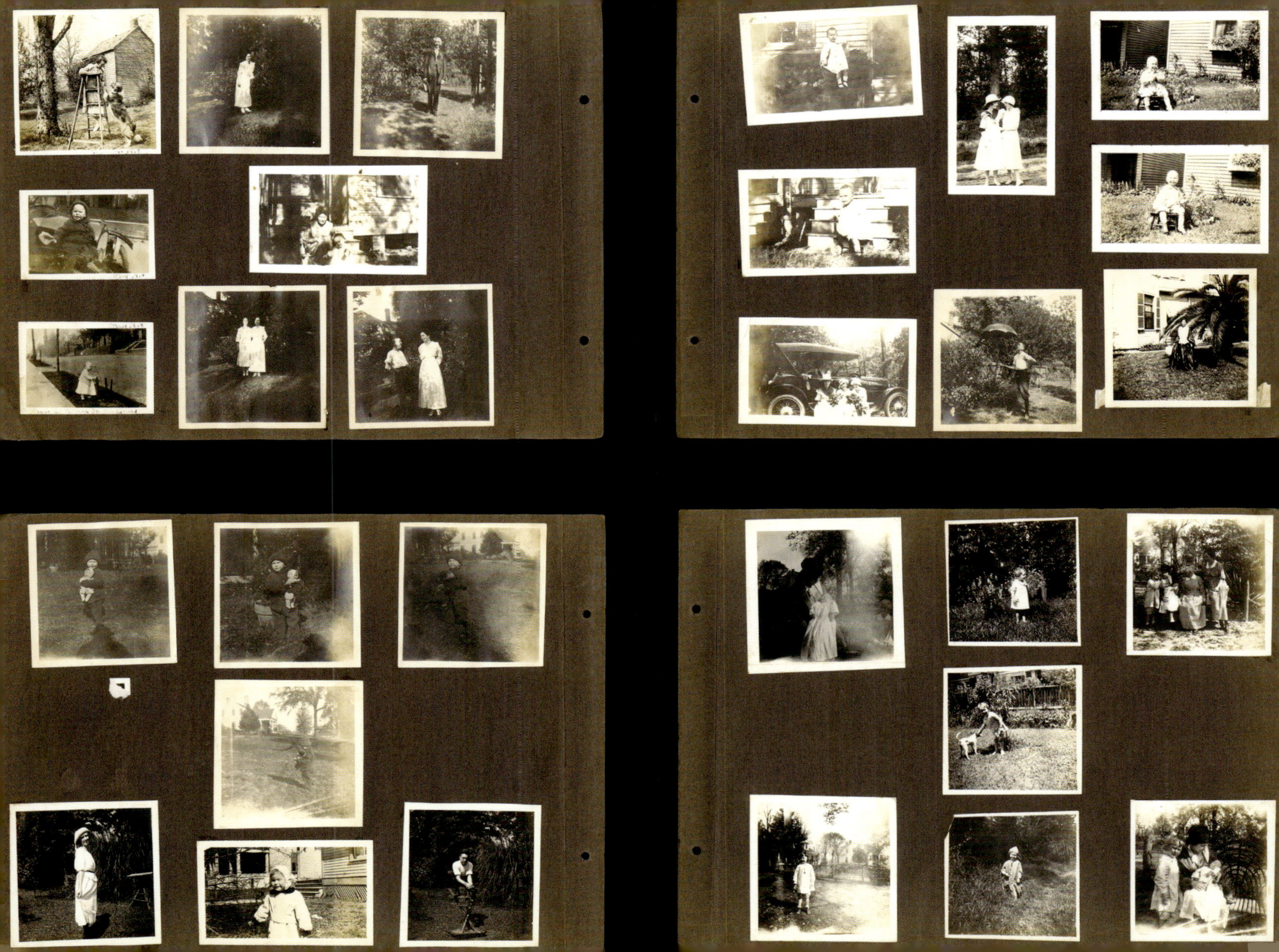

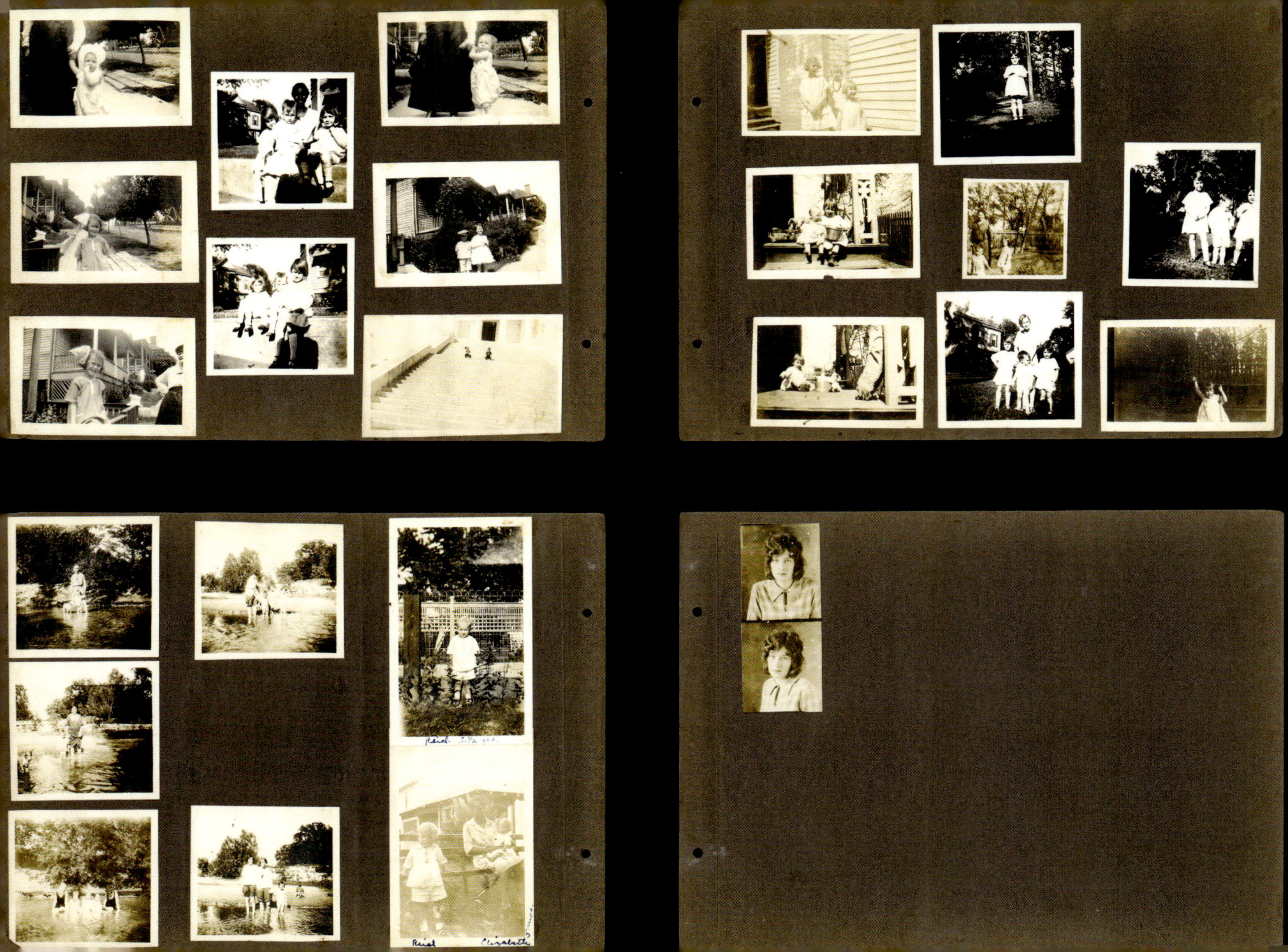
Reid 2½ yrs.
Reid
Elizabeth
3 mos.

Baby's first picture
taken Jan. 26, 1917.
Age sixteen days.
Margaret Gerard Smith
and her Mother —
Taken at Home
624 N. Union St.,
Natchez, Miss.

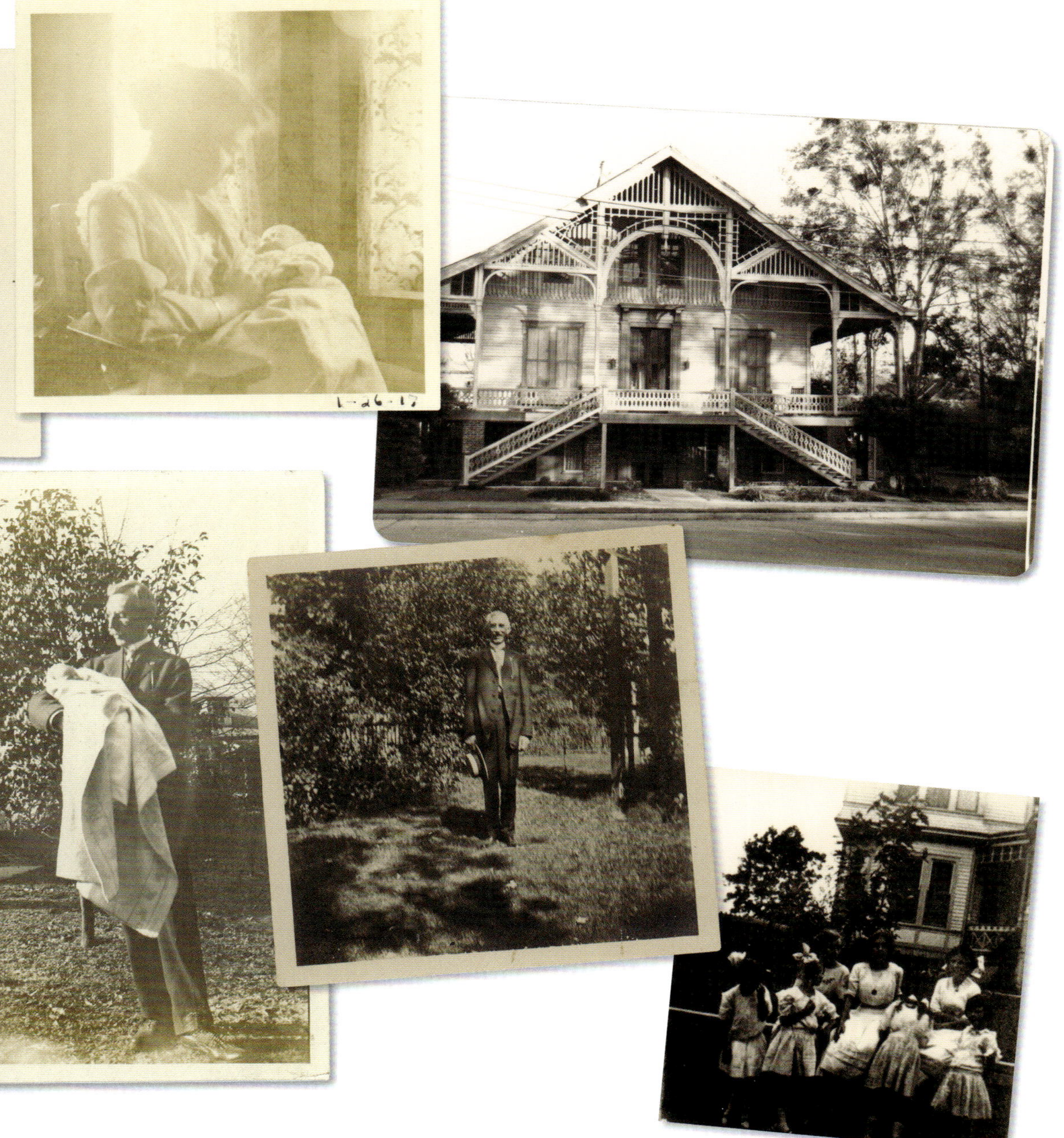

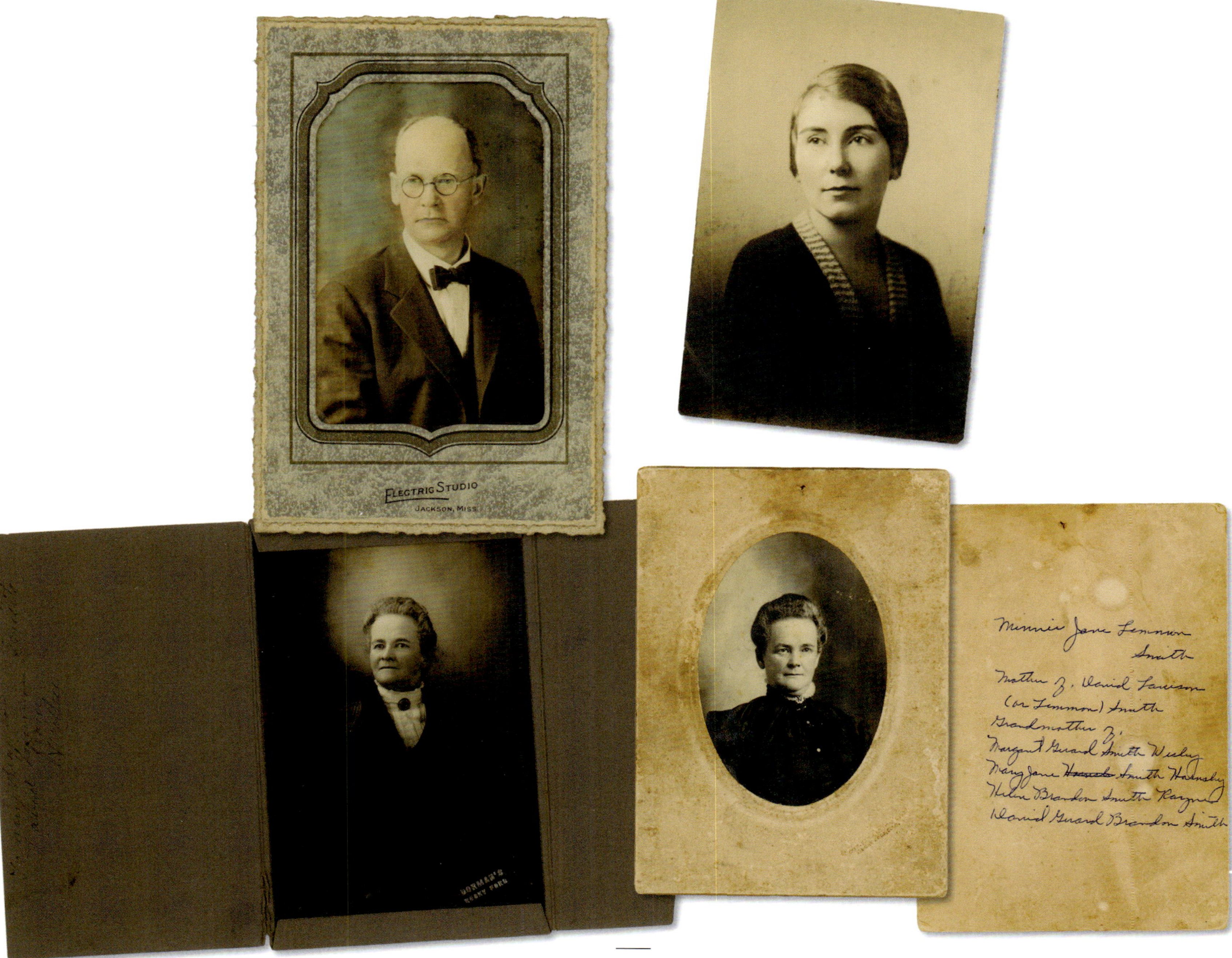
ELECTRIC STUDIO
JACKSON, MISS.
Minnie Jane Lemmon
Smith
Mother of David Lawson
(or Lemmon) Smith
Grandmother of
Margaret Girard Smith Wesley
Mary Jane Smith Hornsby
Helen Brandon Smith Rayne
David Girard Brandon Smith

DR. D. L. SMITH
OPTOMETRIST

WE GRIND
OUR OWN LENSES

THE DOCTOR SMITH
OPTICAL CO.

WHOLESALE AND RETAIL OPTICIANS

Vicksburg, Miss.,
1-10-17

My darling Wife;

I am not in as good sprits to day as I was yesterday for some reason or other I have the blues I suppose it is because you wrote me that you had them, why baby darling I have no intentiön of not coming when you have the baby I have only sent Francis to Gloster and Centerville he is to return friday and I am coming home saturday evening the same as usual then next week I expect to send him to Tallulah and be ready to come home on a minutes notice, I have already sent out my adds saying that I will be in Fayette next Thurs day, so I am going to be there just the same.

Darling as usual when there is somthing that grates on my nerves I go to you for releif, well there is somthing that grates on my nerves now and grates very bad it is a blind man out side singing for the nickels in the fromt of my place I dont think that it is a good thing for business for a blind man to be singinf in front of an optical store, do you. he just had to sing and sing and sing just think of what I have to go through listening to it, ** HORRIBLE**

There is not much to talk about to-night except we did a little over twenty dollars to day which came in as quite a help just now.

I am inclined to think that this is going to be one of my very short letters as I dont seem to be very full of conversation to night and I have such a good time over at Mrs Flippens at night that my night writing after supper has stoped in fact not my writting after supper for I eat supper before going home and then step back in and write some more, but after I go home I have no more writing to do we had a fine time last night talking around the place we made little things to go inf infront of the door Mrs Flippen and Paxton did while we talked.

DR. D. L. SMITH
OPTOMETRIST

WE GRIND
OUR OWN LENSES

THE DOCTOR SMITH
OPTICAL CO.

WHOLESALE AND RETAIL OPTICIANS

2

Vicksburg, Miss.,

I am enclosing Dr Chamberlins letter in answer to the one that I sent him from the tone of it I think that I must have worded it so that it did not make him mad but I hope he dont get in a hurry. when things come off.

I called Francis in to day he drew on me for five dollars more and that was too much I cant stand to have him seeing the country at our expence, So I told Miss Piezza that I would not need her after next week, but will keep her one week longer after this week, so I will keep Francis in the store with me here after and let him go out for one day at a time until he learns to sell a little stuff then I will be able to put him on the road again, and I am kind-a glad to have an excuse to get rid of the lady I dont think much of her.

I do wish that blind man would move up to the next block I am awfully tired of listening to him.

You know sweetness I am tickeled to death over fixing my typewriter only I am not going to die .

Think I will have to cut The thirty dollar saliery that I gave Francis back to twenty five for a while that is if he will stand for it I dont know what to do just now, the only thing that I do know is that I will be in Fayette next thursday and that I will most likely not come back to Vixburg until after the big works is over.

I am going to stop now With a big Kiss I am ,

Your devoted husband,

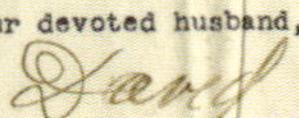

Return after Five Days to
THE DOCTOR SMITH OPTICAL CO.
VICKSBURG, MISS.

VICKSBURG.
DEC 22-17
8—30 PM

Mrs. Ethel B. Smith
% Brandon & Brandon
Natchez, Miss.

Box 265

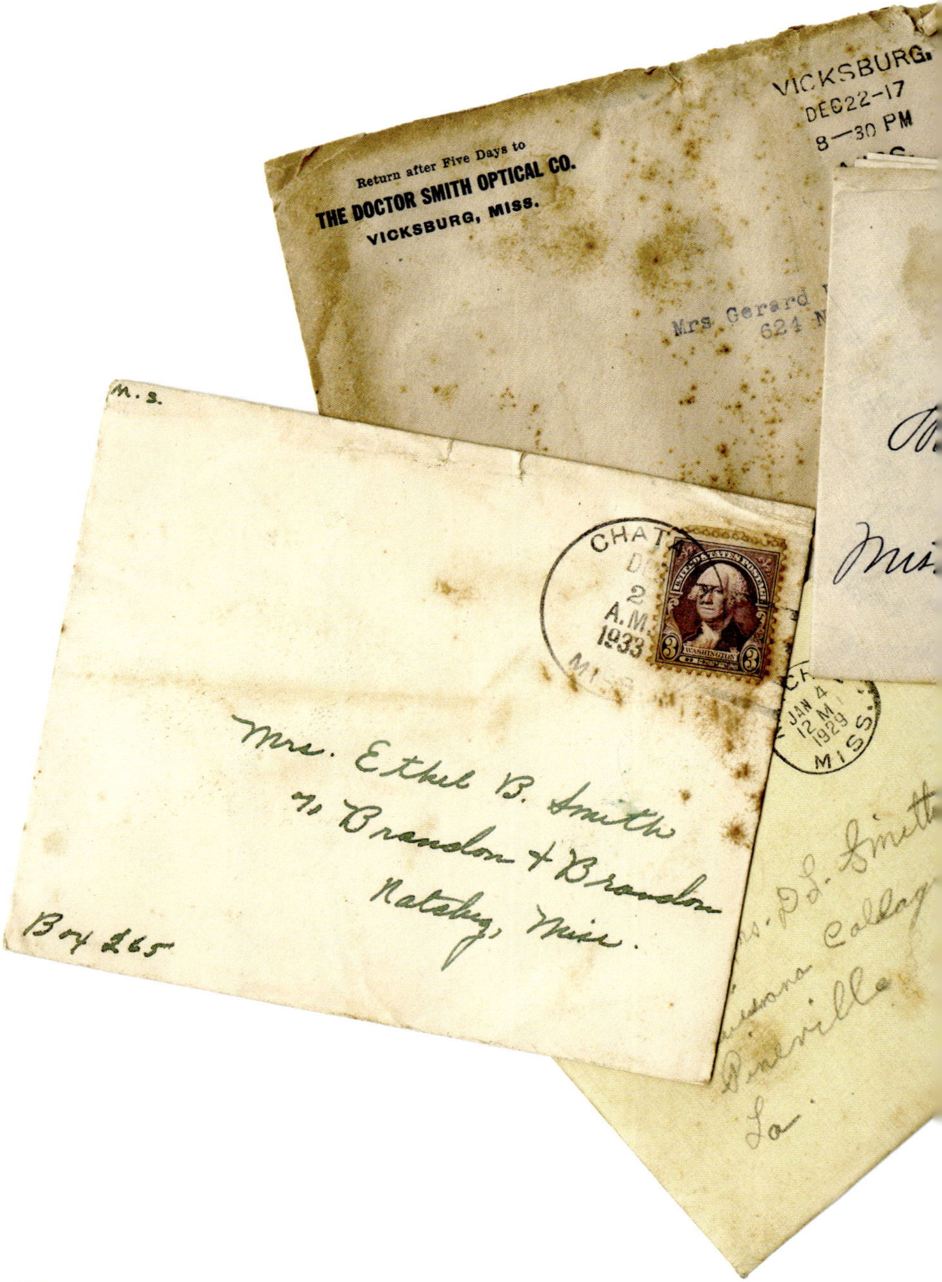

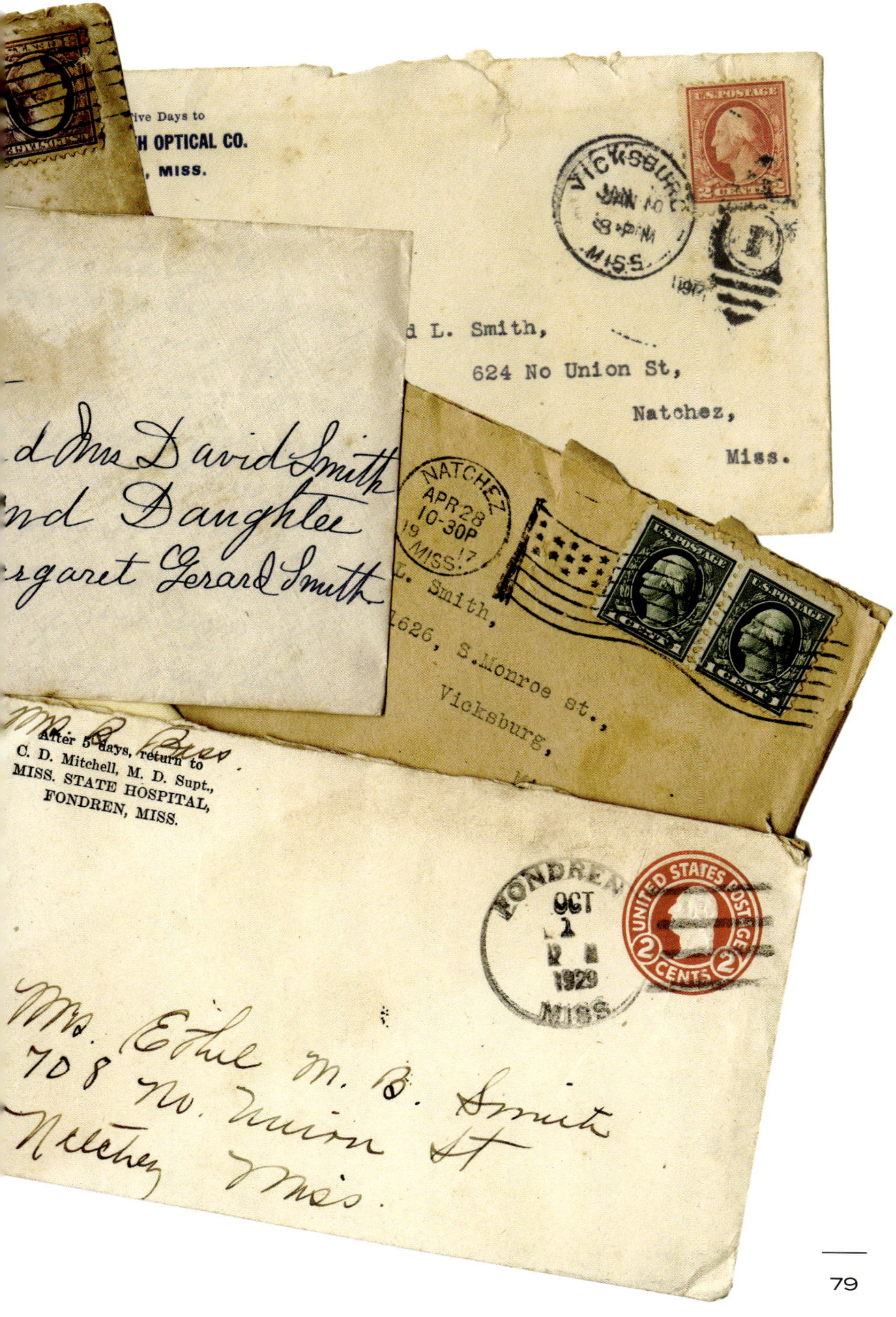

After 5 days, return to
C. D. Mitchell, M. D. Supt.,
MISS. STATE HOSPITAL,
FONDREN, MISS.

Mrs. Ethel M. B. Smith
708 No. Union St
Natchez Miss.

Mr. and Mrs David Smith
and Daughter
Margaret Gerard Smith

L. Smith,
1626, S. Monroe st.,
Vicksburg,

d L. Smith,
624 No Union St,
Natchez,
Miss.

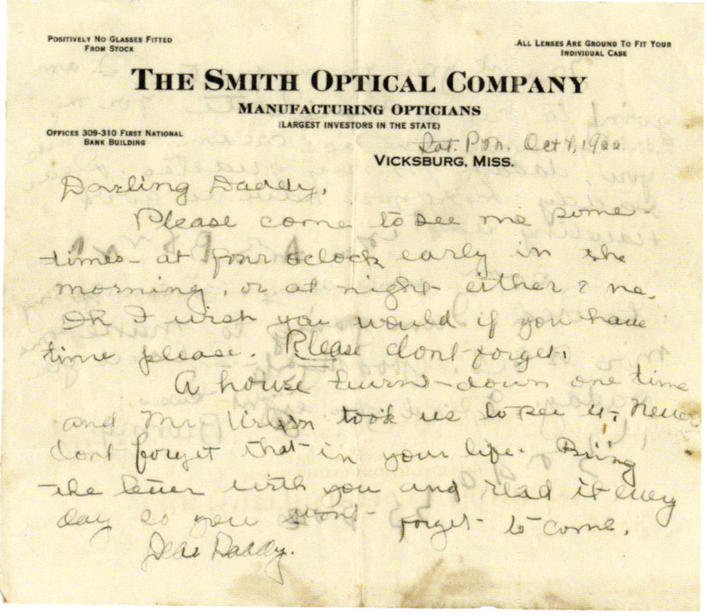

Positively No Glasses Fitted From Stock

All Lenses Are Ground To Fit Your Individual Case

THE SMITH OPTICAL COMPANY
MANUFACTURING OPTICIANS
(LARGEST INVESTORS IN THE STATE)

Offices 309-310 First National Bank Building

VICKSBURG, MISS.

Sat. P.m. Oct 7, 1922

Darling Daddy,

Please come to see me sometimes at four oclock early in the morning, or at night either? no. Oh I wish you would if you have time please. Please dont forget.

A house turned down one time and Mr. Wilson took us to see it. Never dont forget that in your life. Bring the letter with you and read it every day so you wont forget to come.

Dear Daddy.

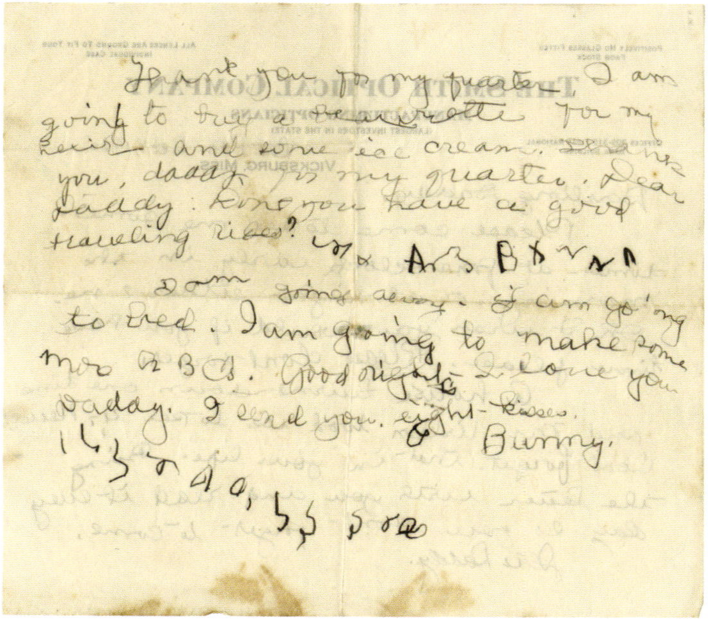

Thank you for my quarter. I am going to buy a barrette for my hair and some ice cream. Thank you, daddy for my quarter. Dear daddy: dont you have a good traveling time?

I am going away. I am going to bed. I am going to make some more A B Cs. Good night. I love you daddy. I send you eight kisses.

Bunny.

Form 1204

CLASS OF SERVICE	SYMBOL
Day Message	
Day Letter	Blue
Night Message	Nite
Night Letter	N L

If none of these three symbols appears after the check (number of words) this is a day message. Otherwise its character is indicated by the symbol appearing after the check.

WESTERN UNION TELEGRAM

NEWCOMB CARLTON, PRESIDENT GEORGE W. E. ATKINS, FIRST VICE-PRESIDENT

RECEIVED AT S. E. CORNER WASHINGTON AND CRAWFORD STS., VICKSBURG, MISS.

18NO B 12

NATCHEZ MISS 451P MAY 10 17

MRS DAVID L SMITH

70

VICKSBURG MISS 1626 MONROE BLVD

PASS VICKSBURG TONIGHT TELL MARTIN CAN YOU AND DAVID COME DOWN TOO

G H BRANDON

456P

708 N. Union St.
Natchez Miss.
Monday, Morning

Dearest grandma,

Mother told me about her devoice the other day from daddy when I was talking about him as I usele do I was telling her how much I would love to see him when she told me I felt like crying I mande me want too see you all the more I am glad to say that Aunt Colner said she was going to bring me down to see her soon and let me come to see you I want you to ask her when you see her next to tell her that the next time she comes to Natchez to bring me to Vicksburg She said she wanted me to come see her soon but I can't come unless she comes and gets me.

To change that subject lets talk of my danceing you will not have too pay for my toe slipers because I saved up the money I got Christmas & what I got on my Birthday + what you have sent me. I bought me a pare stocking + payed my way to the pictures the dollor & seventy cents ($1.70) I had left the stocking were a dollor ($1) but to bring us back to danceing I will tell you how much the danceing slippers cost they cost $5.50 they are very pretty, Miss or Mrs. I realy don't no which but I ought to but I will say Miss Trably said I am a very gracefull dancer. I wish I could find words to thank you I wish I had a picture of you too you are such a dear. I am not saying much but it will do—

Your loving granddaughter
Margaret Smith

P.S. I hope daddy I much better.
P.S. I shall always call you grandma
P.S. I hope you can read this writting

RICH'D F. REED GERARD BRANDON W. C. BOWMAN

LAW OFFICES OF

REED, BRANDON & BOWMAN

NATCHEZ, MISSISSIPPI

Dear Margaret :- This is a picture of the HEN sitting on her NEST in the high GRASS. See the EGGS in the nest.. Do you know your letters yet? You must get Mother to teach you your letters so you can learn to READ and WRITE. The you can read Granfather's letters yourself, and can write a letter to him. If you will come down to see Grandfather and Grandmother when school opens you can go to KINDERGARTEN

HEN

EGGS

GRASS

NEST

GRASS

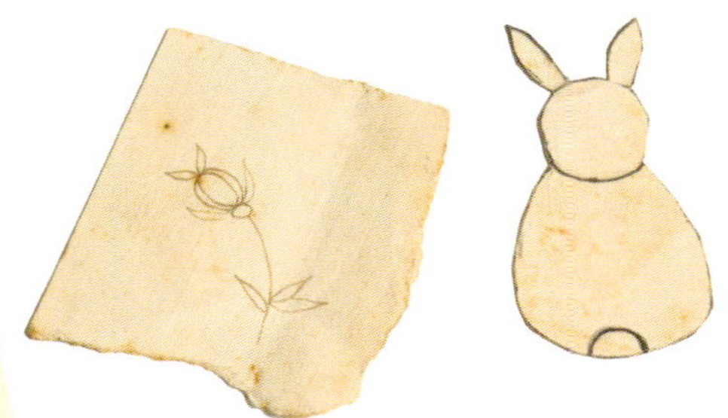

Drew, Miss. Tuesday.

My dear little daughter, mame Ham Bun.

Mother is dressing Helen is laughing and Robt is cooking his breakfast.

It looks like it is going to rain to day cloudy and windy and it's getting cold. I hope you are getting along find and not giving Grand Ma too much trouble. I love you little daughter and hope that some day I will be at home with you always.

I am enclosing you a funny paper. and a quarter treat Mary Jane and kiss her and Grand Ma. for me.

Your devoted,

Daddy.

Miss Margaret Gerard Smith

916 Speed St.

Vicksburg

Miss.

June 25th
We celebrated Ethel's half year birthday with a big "gobbler" for dinner & invited Grandfather & Grandmama & Great Grandmother Patterson out to dine but they could not come much to our sorrow. We had sherbert & cake for dessert but it poured down rain & Mr & Mrs Richard F. Read whom we expected to come to our "jollification" were unable to. So Ethel's "parties" were failures. Much she cared though! —

July 8th 1895
This is a lock of my baby's hair

was she. But when the elephants marched by two by two, her eyes grew bigger and bigger and she quieted down somewhat. The stream of darkies that went by following the wagons seemed to be of as much interest as anything else, she looked as if she was wondering where they all came from.
Up to this time I think she thought the Brandons and Pattersons were the only inhabitants of this sphere! —

Nov 14th 1895
Ethel being eleven months & eleven days old. Is much lighter than when 6 months old.

When Ethel was a baby one of the first objects to attract her attention was the buzzards sailing by overhead. They seemed to fascinate her so that her father composed a lullaby on the subject with which he used to sing her to sleep.

The Buzzard Song
Oh, bye
The baby bye
And see
The buzzards fly
Going by
So high
In the sky
Oh my!
Bye, bye
So bye the baby bye
And shut your little eye
And to sleepy by
To go,
Baby bye.
Bye the baby bye
Bye the baby bye
Bye the little baby bye

whatever toy she has to go to anyone with a book, She will often go and get a book and take it to some one to show her the pictures.

March 13th 1896 —
Fifteen months old —

March 24th 1896
Last Sunday evening after Mr B of [illegible] returned from a [illegible] Ethel was playing with her walking stick — sitting astride it, we told her she was riding her "horsey" and she said no "Bi-cool" (Bicycle). We all thought it so bright and original. I never heard of any other baby saying it. She loves to ride on her uncle "Sam's" (as she calls him) knee, & he & her father often take her up in front of them

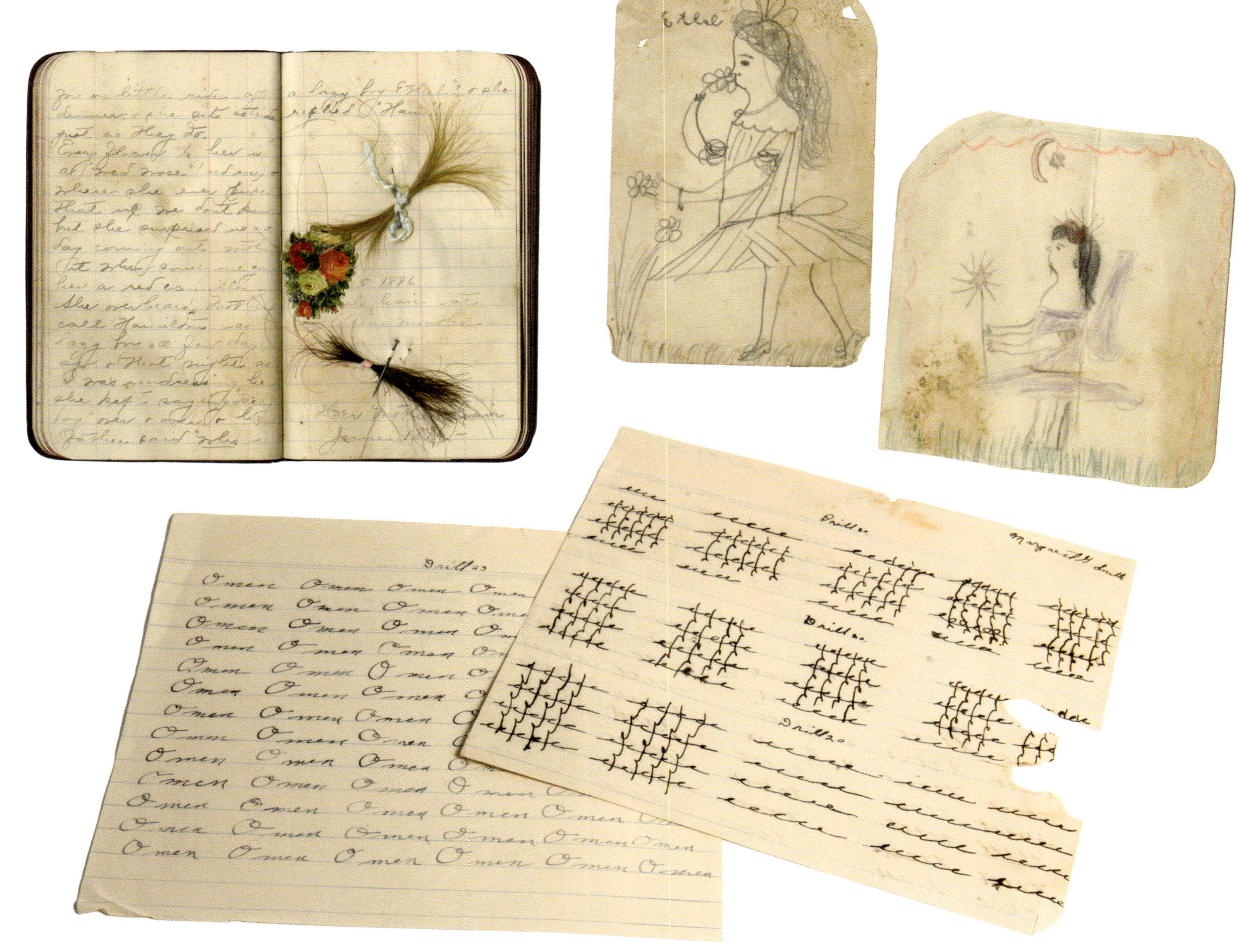

Page 56	*Brochure for the Smith Optical Company, ca. 1915–1924*
Page 57	*Left: Poster advertising the Doctor Smith Optical Company, ca. 1915–1924* *Right: Toy glasses made by Dr. Smith for his daughter Margaret, ca. 1922*
Pages 58–59	*Dr. Smith's traveling case and optometry equipment, ca. 1915–1924*
Pages 60–74	*Family photo album kept by Ethel Brandon Smith, ca. 1910–1930*
Pages 76–77	*Smith and Brandon family photos, ca. 1917–1930s*
Pages 78–81	*Selection of correspondence saved by Ethel Brandon Smith, ca. 1917–1933*
Pages 82–top 83	*Ethel Brandon Smith's baby book and drawings, 1894–ca. 1900*
Page 83 bottom	*Margaret's penmanship drills, ca. 1923*

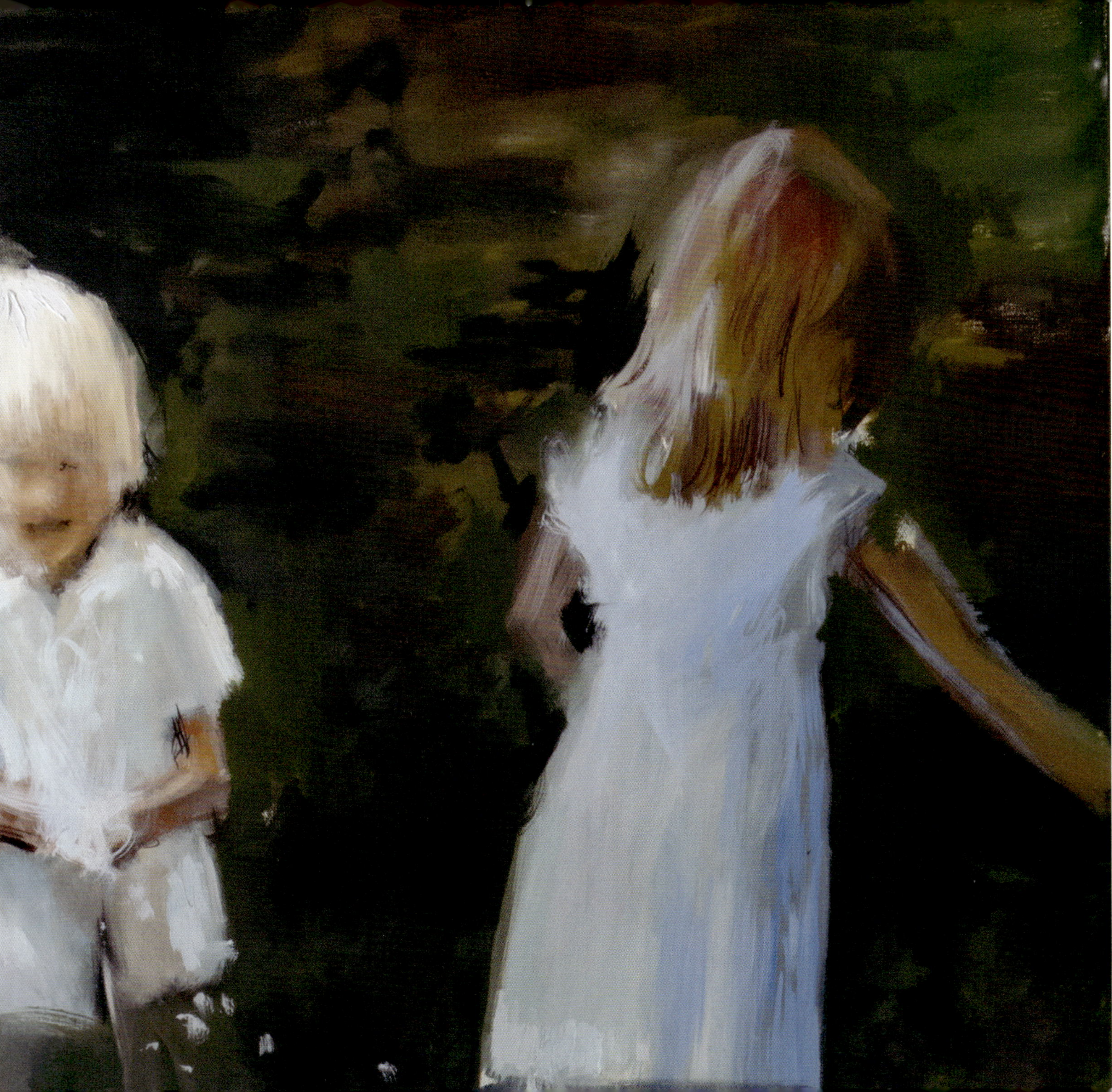

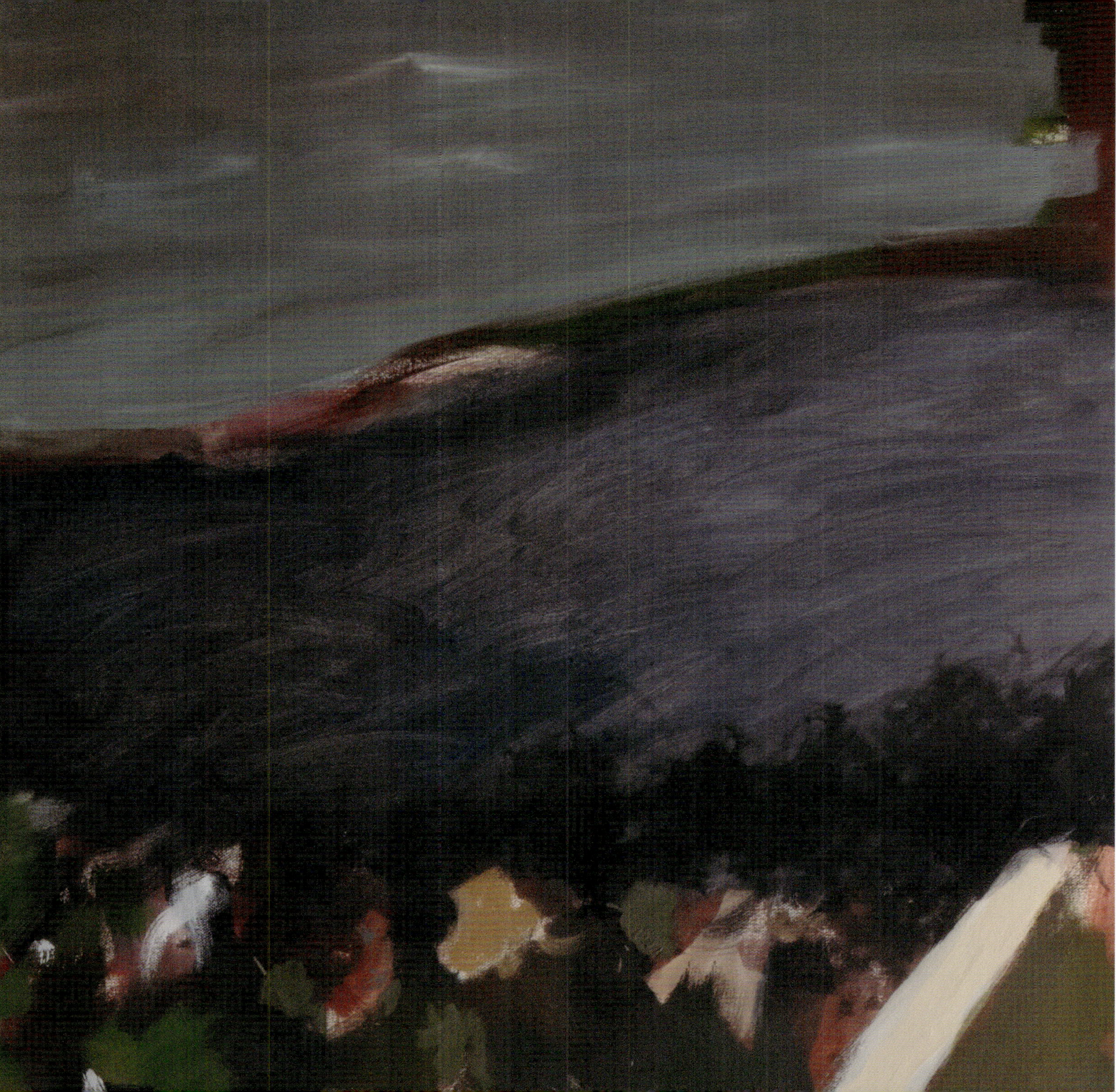

ARTIST ACKNOWLEDGMENTS

I dedicate this catalogue and exhibition to
Margaret Gerard Smith Wesley, who waited.

I WOULD LIKE TO THANK MY WIFE, Julia R. Gordon, for her loving and unwavering encouragement of this project, and for her creative and editorial insights. I could not have seen this through without her support and that of our kids, Vivian, Gus, and Asher.

Uncovering Dr. Smith's story was only possible with the committed research of Stephen Parks, Mississippi's State Librarian, who dedicated his time and energy to this story. Thank you.

Betsy Bradley believed in this project from the day it began, and I thank her for her continued guidance and confidence. I offer my deepest gratitude to Megan Hines, Robin Dietrick, Elisabeth Callihan, Grayston Barron, Jasmine Williams, and all the other wonderful folks at the Mississippi Museum of Art for trusting me and for being reliably insightful, professional, and positive at each stage of the process.

Thank you to Lida B. Gibson, Dr. Jennifer Mack, Dr. Ralph H. Didlake, and Dr. Sara Gleason. My partnership with the Asylum Hill Project at the University of Mississippi Medical Center and their admirable and ambitious work has been a powerfully illuminating aspect of this project.

What Became of Dr. Smith has been actively evolving for seven years. During that time, I have relied heavily on conversations with fellow artists, writers, and musicians who I trust to give honest opinions about and criticisms of the work in progress. Thank you to Timothy Hyman, Ann Patchett, Dan Fortner, Matthew Collings, Jochen Wierich, Stephanie Vogel, and Aimee Mann for your generosity of thought and spirit.

I would like to express my gratitude to my mother, Anna Saterstrom, and the rest of our family, the descendants of Dr. Smith, for their encouragement and openness to my shining a very public light on very private family stories.

Finally, I would like to thank Matthew Burrows and the more than one thousand trusting, supportive people all around the world who bought studies for this work through the Artist Support Pledge. There is no way I would have been able to create this exhibition or catalogue without their help. I am forever indebted.

—Noah Saterstrom

This book is published in conjunction with the exhibition *What Became of Dr. Smith*, on view at the Mississippi Museum of Art April 20–September 22, 2024. *What Became of Dr. Smith* is curated by Megan Hines, PhD, and organized by the Mississippi Museum of Art. This project is made possible in part by the Institute of Museum and Library Services (#MA-251867-OMS-22) and the Center for Bioethics and Medical Humanities at the University of Mississippi Medical Center.

The Mississippi Museum of Art and its programs are sponsored in part by the city of Jackson and Visit Jackson. Support is also provided in part by funding from the Mississippi Arts Commission, a state agency, and by the National Endowment for the Arts, a federal agency.

380 South Lamar Street, Jackson, MS 39201
www.msmuseumart.org

Artwork dimensions are given in inches; height precedes width precedes depth.

Distributed by University Press of Mississippi
3825 Ridgewood Road, Jackson, MS 39211
www.upress.state.ms.us

Editorial management by Robin C. Dietrick, Symmetry LLC, with assistance from Daniel Cook / symmetryllc.us
Designed by Karen Cronin, Cronin Creative / cronincreative.net
Photography of the painting *What Became of Dr. Smith* and its details on pages ii, 3, 7, 21, 32, 33, 44, 45, 54, 86, 87, and 91 by Jerry Atnip.
Photography of archival materials on pages 57, 58, 59, 80, 81, and 83 by Jerry Atnip.

1,000 copies printed and bound in Canada, April 2024.

Mississippi Museum of Art
978-1-887422-24-6

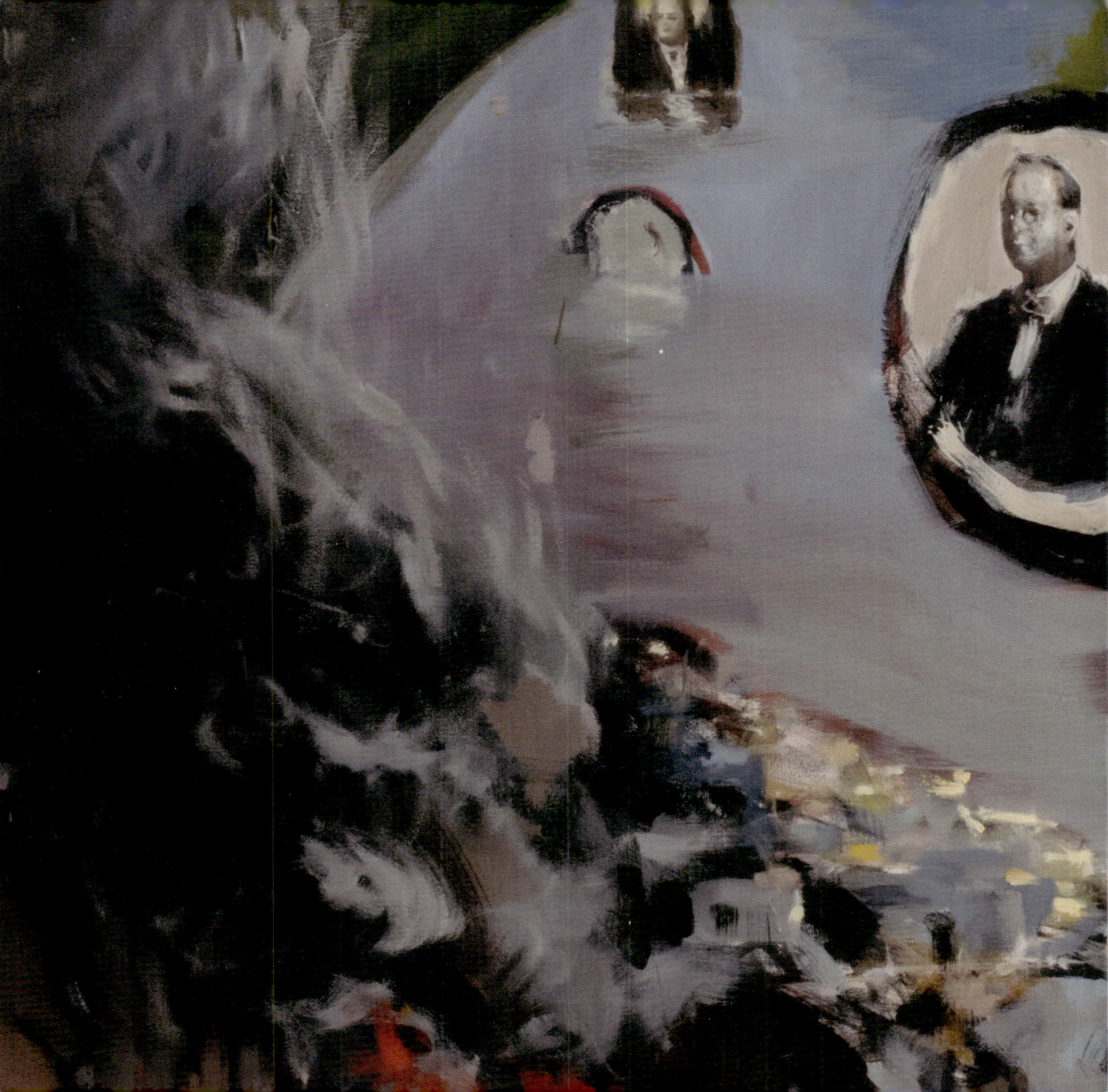

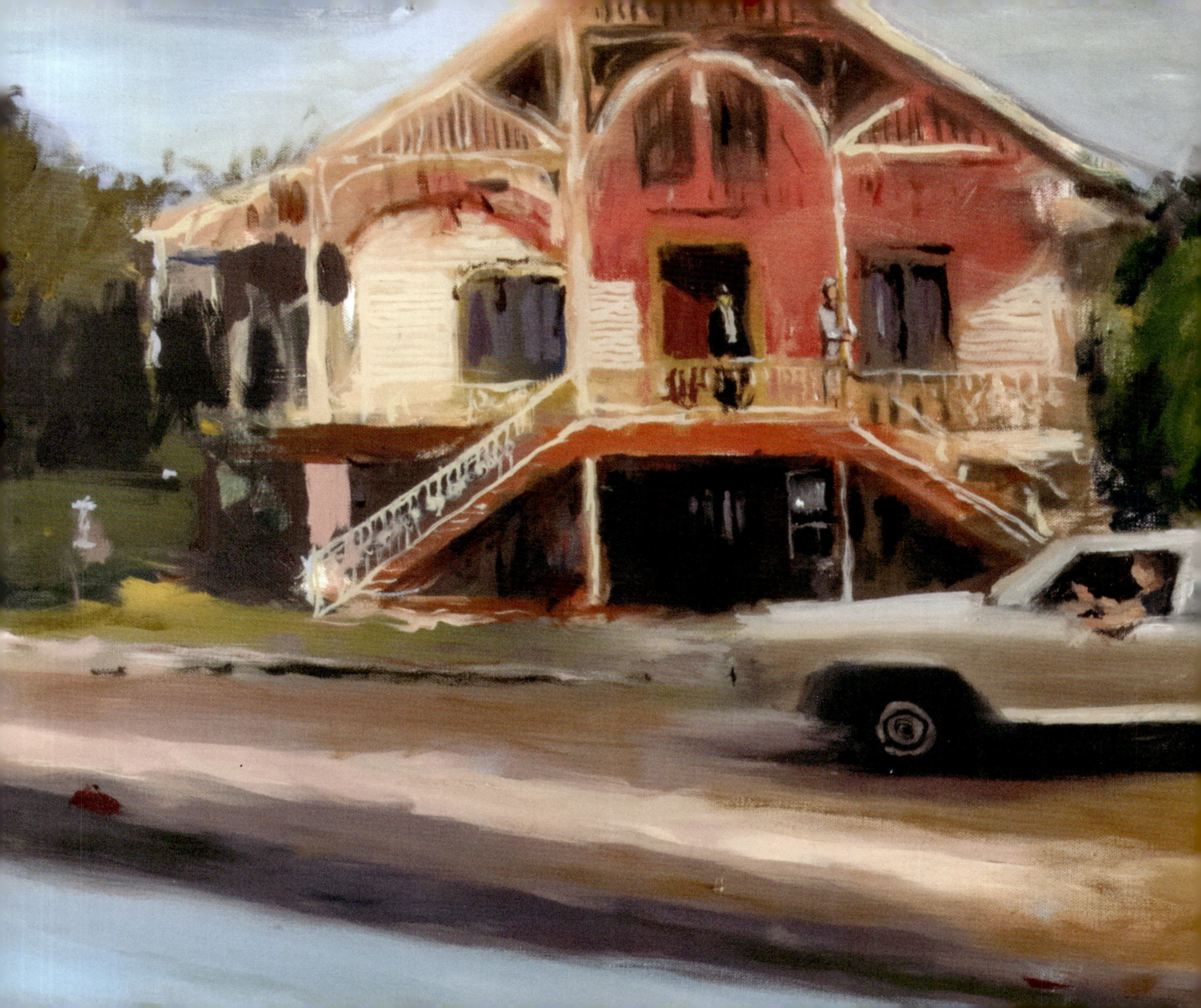